The Refugee
A Novel

Zoltán Böszörményi
Translated from the Hungarian by Paul Sohar

Böszörményi, Zoltán
ISBN: 978-0-7443-2357-3
The Refugee: A Novel / Zoltán Böszörményi – 1st ed.

YourSpecs
An Imprint of SynergEbooks
948 New Hwy 7
Columbia, TN 38401
www.synergebooks.com

Printed in the USA

The Refugee

"The only unforgettable stories are those that happened nowhere."
Friedrich Schiller

The Refugee

"My name? What the hell d'you need my name for?"

The old man leans so close he almost knocks me over with his putrid, garlicky breath. He's apparently waiting for an answer with his mouth left open. He seems upset by my timid yet defiant silence and, most likely, unaware of the steady flow of nauseating stench issuing from his guts.

"You hear me, you dumb jerk? I'm the only one here who asks questions and gives orders!"

The dark shadows in the corners of his eyes reflect the two black teeth sticking out of his mouth. Nevertheless, they do not diminish the fierceness of his glare that's almost blinding me.

But I don't blink. I pretend not to notice this sudden flare up. I think of the trip ahead and take his malodorous verbal lashing without a word. I've already paid his fee; now I have no choice but put up with whatever abuse he wants to heap on me. Maybe that's his professional pride speaking, and I cannot afford to let it upset me. In the next few hours I will need every nerve in my body to concentrate on nothing else but the task at hand. A hike in an unfamiliar landscape spiked with lethal obstacles. Probably just plain farmlands and fields, but they hide a trail that surreptitiously crosses the border, a trail only local guides know about. Like old Blackteeth.

Whatever it is I have to face, I will not back down. I'll show the cantankerous old man what kind of stuff I am made of. No, I'm not going to thwart his will but go around it if I have to; I'm going to look for a path to the vestiges of his humanity.

Nothing about this rancorous character bothers me any longer. Nothing except a sense of shame that jolts me to the very core of my being.

He's got his life at stake. But how about me? What am I gambling with? The thoughts tear into me, wounded as I feel by his treating me like enemy.

But that's exactly what I sound like. If I ask the old man his name, I'm clearly not his friend.

1

Forget it; this is no time to indulge in feelings. We must get going!

In the past to me the word *border* used to stand for an abstract concept, a demarcation line separating two wholly different worlds; one ruled by power without reason and the other by the power of reason. In the former people only dream of freedom, in the latter they practice it every day. The two worlds are deadlocked in a Cold War in which the border between them is an ideological frontline. But now it is about to take on physical reality for me in the form of barbed-wire and machine-gun towers, manned by ferocious border guards whose task is to prevent the citizens from leaving communist utopia. And all that is out there, not too far from here, supposedly a neglected segment of it, cloaked in the black brocade of the night. I don't even know what it is I'm facing, but I have to get to it and somehow manage to slip across. I'm cursed with the misfortune of having been born and brought up on the wrong side of the border, in the world of unreason, in a world that saw an enemy in an innocuous assistant newspaper editor who also happened to be an emerging young poet. A recent night of interrogation by a pair of rather impolite "literary critics" in the cellar of the State Security Agency was not the first and it foreshadowed more permanent accommodation there beside the loss of my job and the livelihood of my young family.

It's no wonder I'm so obsessed, almost running amok; I'm racing against the menacing shadows of my pursuers, and I cannot lose sight of my goal: escape to Austria across the border.

No, I tell myself I have nothing to be ashamed of; I am not running away from a crime, nor from responsibilities. Not even from myself. But as a fugitive from injustice, what else can I do but run?

The old man slowly backs away from my nose. We are at arm's length from each other. I don't even have to look at him.

"Well then, let's get going!" he calls out curtly, like a sergeant used to speaking in terms of commands.

Yes, the world on this side of the border speaks in commands.

He's the one to first step out to the street from this nondescript cottage, our clandestine meeting place. He waits for me to follow before he pulls the door shut. He locks it, too, with a modern small flat key, which he sinks in his pocket, only to check it again, clutching it in his fist. He, too, has his anxieties; it's not his house, not his key, he cannot afford to lose it. Finally, he pulls his hand out with a shrug as if reluctantly putting up with a clumsy habit.

At the corner there's a smoke signal from the muffler of an old rattletrap.

It's raining.

Without hurry though. An easy-going rain.

"Looks like we're in for a real downpour!" He remarks casually, without turning back to me as he takes the seat next to the driver.

I slam the car door shut with a crashing bang. The old man nods, not to anyone in particular, only toward the windshield, maybe in approval of my slamming the door.

Then I realize the nod was intended to the driver who immediately shifts into gear and pulls away from the curb.

We hit the road.

I still can't figure out which route he's going to take.

My fellow travelers who share the bumpy ride with me on the cobble stones know where we're going. To an unnamed village close to the border. I only know their final destination: back to town.

But without me!

They have a reason to return, but how about me?

Now is not the time to answer the seemingly simple question of my returning or not returning; no one expresses any curiosity.

I'm looking at the road. The raindrops smash into the windshield with increasingly loud smacks, like lead balls. Visibility is getting more limited every minute.

The whole thing is beginning to look hopeless.

3

It's really coming down. A real cloudburst.

White arrows crisscross the sky. With their flashes they plow the black clouds. They leave undecipherable graffiti on the dark wall of the night.

Not that I feel like deciphering them. I'm just sitting in the backseat, listening to the wild concert of the storm with the engine noise for ostinato.

My mind is empty. My thinking process has come to a halt. And I make no effort to gather my thoughts.

The old man produces a pack of cigarettes from his pocket. In the faint light of the dashboard I can see the box of matches in his hand, and then I can hear the scratch. The smoke that soon fills the closed car starts to irritate me eyes.

I get the urge to cough, but manage to suppress it, fighting it back down my throat. I feel it's best for me to stay still.

The cross-eyed headlights untiringly scan the road.

Dead souls wandering in a moribund world.

Straight ahead.

"You'd better pay attention to me when we drop you off. I'll tell you only once what to do. If you get it, it's a pretty good bet you'll make it across," the old man turns back to poke me in the arm for emphasis. His voice is sandpaper. Rude, crude and arrogant.

He cannot see that the light has gone out in my eyes and my lips are trembling. He can't feel my icy hands, neither can he see I'm shivering, chilled to the bones.

Rattled by foreboding.

It has just come over me. From nowhere. I had no chance to prepare for it. It takes all I have to clamp down my chattering jaws.

The old man notices none of this.

Neither does he sense I'm in the grips of fear. There's no one to share this with, I'm utterly alone in the car in the company of the old man, his mute partner and the cigarette smoke crawling under my coat.

The home I'm leaving behind comes back to haunt me, the warm bed, my wife, our kids. I have to shoo away the image

4

and steel myself against such tear-jerker notions that can only sap my courage and determination.

Oh God, if you're there, please don't tempt me! Stop torturing me with such seductive thoughts! Save me from myself! I pray in the chapel of my mind, maybe first time as an adult.

If it made any sense, and if someone requested it, I could still squeak a word. Anything's possible.

And yet a few friendly words would mean so much to me now. They could restore my courage and hand me a shield.

The old man is playing a cat-and-mouse game with me like, that's why he stays silent. Or perhaps he senses that there's something extraordinary taking place, and it wouldn't help to disrupt the deadly serious tone of the occasion with chitchat.

Before I notice it we have the outskirt of the city long behind us. I'm in such a state of mind that truly frightens me, in a state that renders a man unable to pay attention to what's happening to him.

I'm sitting here in a crumpled heap, feeling sorry for myself. It's disgusting, I have to admit it.

Next thing is nothing. Even my thoughts turn silent.

"Don't speed!" the old man tells the driver. His voice is rational, calm and almost human. "If you just stay steadily under the speed limit, no one'll pay attention," he adds to his curt command.

The driver straightens out in his seat, tilts his head left and right, like someone feeling stiff and trying to loosen up.

My awareness of the night is so sharp that it could slice mountains.

But only I alone can feel that.

It's my secret. No one else knows about it.

My small brown bag is next to me. It snuggles up to me on the seat. My fingers can trace the edge of a book cover. Yes, I'm taking a Goethe's Faust with me on this dangerous trip.

The car suddenly jerks as the driver steps on the brake, shifting down and then back up again.

"These potholes!" he sighs without adding any more.

Yes, let's think about anything else, but this...

I'd like to see the night but can't make out a thing, it's so dark. Then an enormous thunderclap in the wake of a lightning bolt.

It's pouring. It covers the road, the car, the thick black night. And me, too.

* * * *

The day before I meet old Blackteeth, my hired guide, I'm busy with another important step in the process of my escape. I have to get hold of some convertible currency, something strictly illegal for ordinary citizens to possess and only available in the black market. The safest way to deal with the problem is to approach a bona fide foreigner and offer more than the official rate of exchange. Everybody likes to get a bigger bang for his bucks; tourists tend to shy away from the risk, but foreign students are known to dabble in this financial market. They are easy to find in the bar and the restaurant of the central hotel any time of the day. However, caution is called for; one might run into a police plant. That makes me feel as if facing a roulette table. I could lose my paltry sum if I put it on the wrong number, not that I've ever encountered a real wheel. Nevertheless, I surmise a seasoned gambler is as much obsessed with trying his luck as I am when I have to decide which foreign student to turn to for the illegal transaction.

I place my first bet on the bar.

The cramped and poorly lit place is filled with a thick haze of smoke. I can hardly see a thing.

I give my eyes a minute to adjust to the adverse conditions. At last, I make out three figures seated at the bar.

Two of them are smoking cigars. The short lean one somehow looks trustworthy to me. He's sitting on the high barstool with his legs crossed, leaning on the counter with his left elbow. In his right hand the smoke signal, casually, carelessly like someone performing a ritual rather than enjoying himself.

The pulsing rock music sounds unnatural to me, almost otherworldly, but maybe it's just because the decibel level far exceeds my ears' tolerance.

My target seems totally unaware of his surroundings except for the music. His body shakes in sync with the beat and dips down with the lower notes.

I'm still standing near the door like someone waiting for something or for himself to make up his mind and act.

After an accidental glance at me Shortie slowly shifts his gaze.

The second time he turns to me it's for a long, meaningful look, punctuated with a question mark he draws in the air with the cigar.

I shake my head, no, it's nothing, I want nothing from him, I'm standing here only to listen to the music.

Upon that his burly friend pokes him with an elbow, saying something. The target shrugs, climbs off the barstool and with slow, deliberate steps walks out without looking at me.

I follow him with my eyes and catch his signal to join him as he steps out to the hotel lobby.

It's time to act; suddenly I'm overcome by jitters. What should I do?

Got to go through with it. I head for the lobby.

Shortie is impatiently watching the bar door for me. Catching sight of me he sits down on a leather sofa. He lowers his weight with perfect nonchalance as if he had nothing else on his schedule for the afternoon.

I make my way to the sofa at a strolling pace and take my place next to him in the same leisurely way.

Suddenly he turns to me, takes a powerful drag on his cigar and blows the smoke at me.

"How much do you need?" he asks without any preamble.

"Five hundred," I answer without looking at him.

"My rate is fifty to one," he comes back immediately.

"That's a lot, double the black market rate," I groan with a cramp in my stomach.

"That's my rate. Want it or not?"

"How about forty?" I ask automatically, to my immediate regret; if he's not satisfied with the deal he might report me out of spite. And he can do it with an easier conscience, if indeed it's possible to sell out someone to the police with an easy conscience.

Shortie's silent. Impossible to figure what's going through his mind. Mine is overtaken by worry with rapidly increasing intensity.

"After all, why not?" he seems to be trying to sell himself on the deal.

"All set at forty?" I can't believe the negotiation is over. Maybe I'm missing something.

"I'll expect you at the east corner of the hotel at four. Come alone!"

That sounds a little strange, considering he has nothing to worry about. I'm the one in trouble, in fear of the law. I nod, assuring him of my cooperation.

This incident comes back to me only a week or two later but at an entirely different location. On the other side of the border. I'm standing at the produce market, trying to communicate with the vegetable mongers whose language is foreign to me. Again, the issue is currency, I wonder if they can accept the one I'd bargained for with so much trepidation. One old woman turns to me speaking my native tongue: "How can I be of help to you, young man?"

* * * *

Shortie's waiting for me at the agreed time and place. He looks at least ten years younger in the casual clothes he's changed into. He's got a zippered sweatshirt on. He's casually holding a small gym bag. He appears to be waiting for a girlfriend for a date that probably involves workout at a fitness center, followed by sauna, dinner, privacy in his apartment and finally sex.

As soon as I catch sight of him, I feel a smile coursing across my face; his eyes light up on seeing me. Yet I'm trembling from head to toe, expecting the guardians of the law to swoop down on me and arrest me for currency speculation.

This state of nerves has been with me ever since I laid my eyes on Shortie and it stays with me until I finally get out of the stinky drinking hole where he guides me to finalize our transaction. But by then the five hundred is safely tucked away in my pocket, in twenty-mark denominations. What a relief! I can't believe this phase of my adventure is over.

It turns out Shortie's a real gentleman. He's satisfied with thirty-eight to one conversion rate. This unexpected turn of events leaves me with extra spending money.

Returning to my room I take inventory of my total resources. I pull up a corner of the wall-to-wall carpet and place my small stack of bank notes under it. The result of my assessment is that the extra amount should cover the cost of a nice dinner and even a drink or two in the nightclub next door.

At this point I can't help questioning the wisdom of visiting a nightclub when tomorrow I am to take the most decisive step of my life. Of course I am longing for relief from the tension that was lit up inside of me a few days earlier. I've been giving in to all temptations ever since and even inventing new ones.

New temptation? I ask myself in the mirror, but the only answer I can come with is a faint frown.

* * * *

It's important to remember that the last few days in my homeland were very hard on mey nerves. Up to the moment I ran into old Blackteeth I had the feeling I was fighting a losing battle. This feeling went well beyond a rational assessment of my situation; it was born out of some inner force, a part of me I could not shake off. I could've done it easily in that cellar by signing a statement and naming some names, but I didn't. And not because I was a hero or wanted to become one, but because I simply froze up and could not have cooperated with my interrogators even if I'd wanted to. At the end a face, badly in need of a shave, came very close to mine and warned me in a gravelly tone never to talk to anyone about that night. I think I actually started weeping for some reason, and the next thing I knew it was morning, and I was in our street, walking home.

It was not until the following night that I could get a good night's rest. When I woke up the next morning I had only fuzzy recollections of the night in the cellar, but one thing was very clear to me: the world was lying in ambush for me, and I had to go on a pre-emptive attack, all the while building up my confidence in my ability to deal with any situation and anyone it may involve. An inner voice whispered to me that I could do it, I could come out with flying colors from the upcoming test of my abilities and resolve.

Nevertheless, once in a while I turned numb and debilitated, like someone suffering from a lingering illness of the soul without a cure in sight. Actually, in the short space of time available to me I had no chance of curing it but I could relieve it of the burden weighing me down.

That was the reason for my being on the run, blindly and obsessively. Quarry chased by everyone around, including myself.

And another thing about old Blackteeth: by withholding his name he illuminated the state of mind in which someone outside of society is condemned to operate. No names. No identities. No ideologies. No value systems at all. Just plain existence. That was exactly how I reacted to my escape, but to such an extent that I was not even aware of it as it was happening. I automatically made up names – *nome de guerre* – for everyone I met, starting with the *Lager – Regal*.

* * * *

More about the night before my daring adventure.

I drag myself back to my room. When I open the door, I find Shortie facing me with a sour smile twisting his dry lips. He's here to check on me, see what I'm up to. Curiosity is animating him, but not enough to question me as to the purpose of the converted currency.

He's just smiling. No need to speak.

He suspects it's no point asking me; I'll keep my secret. Instead, he assumes my pitifully enacted enigmatic pose. If we keep studying each other's faces much longer, we'll break out laughing, doubling up helplessly. Then, as inexplicably as he had appeared, he suddenly vanishes.

Hallucination?

The cheap room has one single bed, a night table and a closet. Taking off my shoes and jacket I hit the bed still dressed for street.

That's how I pass the time until the evening.

* * * *

"If you don't keep your eyes on those lights," old Blackteeth points toward a row of bright pinpricks in the dark, still far away, "you'll get off the path going across the border and double back to where you started from. Make a good note of this. Always keep those lights in your sight, those lights over there!"

Rain water is running down the sleeve of his jacket. He doesn't shake the raindrops off even though they've soaked through the fabric. I can't actually see it, but I figure the same is happening to me. I can feel the horrifying coldness of the rain seeping through my light linen jacket.

The old man turns to get back into the car without a farewell. I'd like to crawl back to the backseat, but I can't make a move. I'm just standing there, rooted to the ground.

Can't take a step forward or back.

In the faint light of the dashboard the outlines of the old man's stolid face stand out. That's the last I see of him. But the thing that occupies my mind is not that, but with obsessive

11

curiosity I wonder what's going through his mind. If anything at all.

The driver lets the engine growl softly as he makes a K turn on the narrow dirt road like a ghost, only a few meters from the spot that holds me by my newly sprung roots.

The arc of a light beam leaps out of the dark and splits the sky in half. It lights up the black-clad terrain. Without even thinking about it, I dive into the cornfield lapping the road. I don't even wonder how I've suddenly regained my mobility.

I crouch among the cornstalks. I have sore muscles in my legs and my feet are developing blisters. Yet I haven't taken more than ten steps. It's time to get moving.

Lightning bolts quickly follow one another, releasing deafening thunderclaps from the night sky. The dance of the fireworks slowly moves on, but the symphony of the sky stays on molto crescendo.

How can anyone see me in the midst of this storm? My nerves settle down slowly. Ready to go.

But the tall cornstalks obstruct my vision; I can't see the lights I am supposed to keep in my sight.

How am I going to find my way to freedom?

I don't even notice it when my blood circulation gets back to normal and my calves regain their strength.

At long last, at the edge of the cornfield, the lights the old man pointed out gradually come into my view again. The darkness separating me from them is now sinking back into silence. I make my way in that direction whatever it is I have to wade through. Wet corn is replaced by wet branches, but they keep snapping at me all the same.

They hurt only my thoughts, not my body.

I do not stray from my course.

No brambles, no slimy ditches can halt my progress.

I must make it to the other side.

* * * *

Once I am safely across the border, I bitterly scold myself for having neglected to send my aunt a letter preparing her for my surprise visit. It's been decades since we last saw each other, but she's the only person in Austria with some familial ties to me, someone to show me the ropes. Unfortunately, I only have her address in the town of Linz, but no phone number. I have to take several buses to get there, all the time trying to look nonchalant, but the ravages of the border crossing and the sleepless nights soon make me look like homeless wino. I find the best way to deal with the suspicious glances of the cops is not by running away from them but by ignoring them, acting like a student bumming his way through Europe.

Finally, I'm in the town of Linz and hopefully at the right address. I push the buzzer at the front entrance of her apartment house. She doesn't quite understand who the visitor is, and she only lets me in as far as the door to her apartment. But she keeps me waiting there for long minutes, because she doesn't recognize me through the spy hole. She asks me several times who I am. Then she checks me out by questioning me about the details of memories we have in common before the door opens at last.

On seeing me in life size she claps her hands in dismay. "My God, what's happened to you? You look awful!" she keeps repeating as if seeing a ghoul.

She makes me take off my shoes and my jacket, still wet inside from the rain, and wash my hands before she leads me to the kitchen. She produces beer and cold cuts from the refrigerator. While building a sandwich for me she keeps asking me about every detail of my adventures. She relives with me the storm, the scary run across the border, the trip by bus and the searching looks of the railroad policemen.

I am pleasantly full when she orders me back to the bathroom, handing me towel and pajamas. In the living room she makes a bed for me on the floor. She apologizes repeatedly for the lack of available extra bed in the apartment.

Next morning during breakfast she makes me repeat the whole story of my trip. She's so insistent in her questioning that I get the feeling I am not in her kitchen but at a precinct house. At the end she informs me she has plans for me.

Years earlier a member of the family immigrated to Australia. That's where I should make my way, she announces in a tone that brooks no opposition.

I nod in agreement.

Without further delay we jump into her car and drive to the Australian embassy.

It's a distance of one hundred and forty kilometers to Vienna. Plus, it takes an hour just to get through the center of town. It wears me out. It's not the drive but the fear of the unknown and the unnamable apprehensions associated with it that weigh heavily on my mind.

We walk to the gate of the embassy in pleasant, early fall sunshine.

My relative explains to the security guard what our business is. He listens patiently and ushers us into a waiting room. In a short while a middle-aged lady asks us into her office. My relative goes through my story and my request again; she would like me to travel to Australia immediately.

The official produces a thin smile and shakes her head.

"Impossible, my dear lady," she explains gently, like talking to a child, "for that, the young man needs a permission to enter the country. And there's only one way to secure that. He has to report to the detention camp for undocumented refugees, at the Regal in Traiskirchen. That's where he can apply for immigration permit and wait it out."

She repeats the last sentence twice before she stands up to escort us outside.

My aunt and I, we both agree I should move in expeditiously. Tomorrow. No time to waste.

* * * *

14

The very next day my aunt drops me off at the first station in the processing of an undocumented alien: The Camp. Or Lager as the uniforms at the checkpoint by the wrought iron gate refer to this sprawling and rather nondescript complex of old structures located in Traiskirchen, a small town about twenty kilometers from Vienna. As I am to learn soon, it was built at the turn of the century to house a military academy for the Hapsburg Monarchy in its heyday. After the disastrous WWI the once glorious Monarchy was reduced to Austria which, stripped of its chattel nations surrounding it, had no more need for the military school. The big old institution then served various purposes until after WWII when it became a DP camp, or *lager* in German, a camp for displaced persons, as refugees were called back then. What are we called now? Refugees? Mostly just illegals or undocumented aliens, at best. I wonder what kind of a crowd I'm about to be thrown in. Well, I tell myself I can put up with anything so long as I'm safe. And these plain but massive walls hold promise, at least in that respect.

But somehow I don't like the sound of the word *lager*... What choice do I have? Ever since I started running, I've accepted the terrain I had to cross in my headlong run. Lager? Just another hurdle in the obstacle course to freedom. My mind automatically inverts the ominous word to Regal, and from then on that's what I hear whenever someone mentions lager. The gorgeous view of high mountains in the distance justifies the nickname, the name Regal, usually given to luxury hotels.

* * * *

The officer in charge of Reception is curious and wants to chat, but I have no tales to tell, no mission accomplished to report, no ingeniously worked out escape plan to reveal. I'd barely thought it over before I set out for the unknown. It's a good thing too I have little to say, because my nerves are still so overwrought that I can hardly speak. I must seem some kind of a nut case, fleeing not only from my homeland, The

15

Carpathians, but from a lunatic asylum; the truth is I'm still shaking. A part of me is still running.

Bending over a large map of a small corner of Eastern Europe with a sharp pencil in one hand, the lieutenant traces a line.

"Here?" he asks pointing at a faintly marked spot.

I lean closer to read the name of the village.

"Yes," I say, eager to help, as if it was a big load off my mind, and yet all I'm doing is trying to say something intelligible by confirming a detail of my adventures prior to my sitting there.

My palm is damp. I can see the gleam of the tiny sweat beads there. I wipe them off on the sides of my pants.

"So that was the great escape?" the officer raises his eyes at me, sitting down on his side of the desk.

I can't open my mouth, let alone give an answer. Still numbed, I keep staring at the map. At that certain spot. A dot that marks the end of my life as I had planned it before taking off on this run. Have I reached my goal? Can I stop running now? Yes, I've arrived at the unknown. But what does that mean? One thing is sure: I'll be in limbo, my life on hold for the foreseeable future.

* * * *

The officer is done with me. He digs up a pack of cigarettes from a pocket of his stiff uniform.

He pulls one out.

Sticks it between his dry lips.

Looks at me.

Holds the pack out for me with a clumsy gesture.

I politely decline.

The flare lights up his face. On the right cheek he has an old scar I have not noticed earlier. But of course, I haven't had the time to observe him. I've been preoccupied with myself.

The officer dials a phone.

From the other end a barely discernible voice floats by me.

The cigarette smoke irritates my eyes. It makes them tear. I try to mop up the teardrops surreptitiously.

After a short conversation he replaces the receiver, rises from the chair and signals to me with the cigarette to follow.

Doors open one after another leading from one drab office to the next, until we finally reach a long, high-ceilinged corridor. It echoes emptiness; not one of the doors comes alive with a busy administrator rushing through or a resident coming out to greet me.

Maybe I'm in the wrong place. Or they move people to other countries at a very fast pace. That may be the reason why we don't encounter a soul in the old labyrinthine building, the old cadet school now demoted to the rank of a *lager*. As such, the originally Spartan structure, built for the purpose of teaching discipline with the total disregard of aesthetics, has obviously fallen on hard times. It shows severe signs of neglect, which makes it now look even more like a penal institution, and the absence of human inhabitants only darkens the bleakness of the walls, decorated by nothing but marks of peeling paint.

The officer walks a few steps ahead of me. He has a soft, athletic gait, almost graceful. The rubber soles of his boots produce an eardrum-teasing *yisss-yisss-yisss* sound, searing its rhythm into by brain.

He stops in front of a door to the left and waits for me to catch up before entering a large storage room filled with shelves.

He leads the way to a counter and greets the young man behind it. Explains I'm a new arrival he has to escort to the holding pen as soon as I am supplied with bed sheets, towels, toiletry articles, etc.

The young man stares at me; not long enough to bother me, at least not by his own judgment. But then he remarks in a low tone.

"Don't worry, you're in the right place. That is if you've come to this country without a visa or passport. But watch out for yourself in the holding pen…"

17

I thank him, and he places a file on the counter and copies my name from the documents brought by the officer. Then he gets to work, in a few seconds he collects the requested items from the shelves. He drops them on the counter without comment; pillow case, sheets, blanket, soap...

My escort waits patiently, leaning by one arm on the counter. He remains silent.

Before I know it we're all done.

The stockroom clerk has nothing more to say but does produce a thin smile for dismissal.

Time for me to assume my role in this little drama; I scoop up the stuff from the counter and follow the officer back to the long corridor.

The same eardrum-teasing *yisss, yisss, yisss...* Still no one coming toward us or following us.

The desolation of the place elicits an unpleasant echo in my head, the mood of a bleak end-of-the-world scenario.

The officer walks a few steps ahead.

At the end of the corridor we stop at a door that has opaque glass windows protected by steel bars. My guard presses a button on the side of the door jamb. Within seconds there's a muffled click in the lock.

Next, we're in a staircase, going up. After the first landing I notice brown spots of various sizes splattered_on the stone steps. They look very much like dried blood to me.

The officer stays close to me now. We mount the steps in unison.

He must see what I see.

But he has no comments.

Beyond the next landing the wounded wall carries the signs of scattered shots in the plaster.

Shots like these can be fired only from a submachine gun, I observe silently to myself.

My escort seems to catch on to the urgency of the questions going through my mind.

"Last week there was an insurrection in the Regal," he explains without stopping.

In the door of the next landing the glass plates, reinforced with steel mesh, are riddled with bullet holes.

I tighten my grip on my bundle of bed sheets.

"Most of the rebels have been moved to a high-security facility, but a few of them are still with us. You'll have to share a cell with them, but these are the less boisterous ones," he explains while pressing another buzzer by another bar-secured door.

The same muffled buzz, followed by a click. We step into another corridor.

"This section is the Regal's prison. We call it a holding pen," the officer opens the door to an office and drags me in with him. "All newcomers must stay in this locked unit while their applications for asylum are examined and investigated. If and when they are approved, they are released into the general population of the Regal. But first, the bad apples must be separated from the rest, and we get all kinds here coming across the borders."

"But where is the general population?" I wondered in my confusion.

"Out on the town, or the park, wherever they want to go… And it's weekend, all the offices are closed, there are no interviews, no applications handled, no business conducted. That's why the other floors are quiet now. The place will be buzzing soon when they come back for the night. Once you get a Regal card, you'll be able to move to the open floors and come and go as you please."

In the meantime, though, indeed it's more like a prison scene.

Two uniformed men sit behind as many desks. One of them has a submachine gun hanging from his shoulder. Apparently, he is about to take off.

"A new jailbird for you guys," my escort announces tartly to his colleagues.

They give me a deprecating smile.

Standing in the middle of the office I must look like haplessness personified. I feel all conscious control seep out of my muscles.

My mind is numb. So is my body.

My limbs must be mobilized by a force unknown to me. I can see and hear everything that happens around me, but none of it registers in my mind.

"Put him in cell 28," my friendly reception officer instructs the office personnel, turns around and goes out the door without as much as looking at me.

* * * *

At the Regal, still unsettled, still with the necessities of my detention draped over my arms, I hear my escort's voice as he takes his leave of his submachine-gun-toting colleague.

"Don't forget tomorrow's party. Bring the missus, too. I want no excuses, no sick children at home, none of those fairy tales."

I'm still standing in the guard room.

Clutching the bed sheets.

Waiting for the next officer in charge of me to lead the way.

He shoos me out to the corridor.

We're on the top floor of the building. Ideal place for the locking up people, but why lock up everyone just to screen out occasional criminal elements? I only hope it's not for long. I decide to take it like having to go through a metal detector.

The officer leads me to the third room – and at that point I always make my mind go blank, I erase all recollection of entering the large room filled with steel-framed cots. Neither do I want to recall what activities the denizens were engaged in.

Most of the time I succeed in suppressing the film frames of that first night at the Regal to the extent that they are not accessible to my memory, too deeply enshrined in fog where they lose their contours and become unidentifiable.

I can only go on with my life by resisting them.

20

But sometimes I let them emerge from the fog.

I can see myself standing with the bundle issued to me downstairs in the middle of the room, which turns out to be larger than a cell—as I envision a prison cell—it looks more like a small dormitory, a place originally designed to accommodate cadets during their rigorous training to become officers of the Habsburg Empire. Perhaps the purpose of the building explains why it could never be spruced up and made more welcoming.

* * * *

While following the guard to the cot he picks out for me, a story from my childhood flashes across my mind.

The boarding school where I went also operated the public library. The librarian in charge was a balding, sixtyish gentleman. He was a chain smoker. Every time I visited the place I had to wait for the smoke cloud to dissipate before I could make out his robust figure behind the desk. As a teenager I looked upon him as the king of books; anyone in possession of so many books must be an absolute ruler. His name was Albert.

I always knocked before entering, took off my regulation school cap and greeted him politely. And loudly, in case he could not see me through the smoke.

Eventually he took notice of me. I pulled myself up, standing at attention and watching every move he made.

When he deemed it was time, I had spent waiting sufficient, he gave me permission to pick out a book with a leisurely wave of his hand toward the shelves.

Usually I had four or five books to check out. Albert entered the title and author of each with his meticulous handwriting on a yellow cardboard and handed them to me without a word. On one occasion he stopped the usual routine and carefully examined 18one of my selections, "I Was a Doctor in Auschwitz" by Miklos Nyiszli. He looked at it front and back, flipped open a few pages and then asked me with sad curiosity.

"A horrible book. Why do you want to read it? It's about war, concentration camps and lagers."

I grabbed the book from his hand and opened it at the pictures. "See?" I pointed at one." That's why. I want to exorcise the spirit of fear from my soul."

* * * *

The truth is, some nights are nigh impossible to forget. Not so much the ones filled with mystery or life-changing events but the nights charged with horror; they are the ones that sear themselves into our consciousness and remain only thinly veiled by the persistent fog of pain. Or else it's my fault that sometimes, especially when overwhelmed by new impressions, I am unable take in everything around me as if my mind were partially blindfolded. The word prison frightens me. Perhaps that's why I blindly follow orders instead of assessing my new surroundings.

My last escort points to a bare cot.

"Here," he grunts, and he's already walking out. The rubber soles of his boots let out a scream on the high polish of the floor.

The cot is a basic model, made out of bent steel pipes. On it is a badly spotted mattress. Finally, I can unburden myself of the stuff I've been carrying. I unfold the sheet, spread it out and tuck the ends under the mattress, all four sides, like I learned in boarding school. It has to be as tight as a sail on a mast. In no time at all I'm done and proceeding to spread the other sheet and then the blue-and-white striped blanket over it. Job well done, I start straitening up and... *blam*! I feel a tremendous blow on my left shoulder followed in a few seconds by another one on the back of my head, both from the hand of an unseen foe behind me.

I freeze.

Here come the bad apples!

Waiting for the next blow.

Nothing.

The silence seems to be winning.

The ceiling light dims as if in step with the desperate situation.

The Windows too have frozen up.

I'm still afraid to turn around and face my attacker.

Hoarse growls plow into the gelled air and trail off as howls of laughter.

"Now, now, welcome!" a voice from the far corner of the room.

I turn around.

Repeated howls.

A skinhead of average height is showing his wide back to me, nonchalantly walking away, his head swaying like a melon.

I wish I could at least see his face.

With loping, oafish gait he joins his fellows who are by now screaming with frightening hilarity.

One of them wields a gleaming butcher knife of enormous proportions in his hand. He swings it around and then raises it above his head. Even in the dim light the reality of the wide steel blade is unmistakable.

"Take it easy, sonny boy, we just wanted to give you a proper welcome... You moved in here in such a great hurry you forgot to say hello to us. Now, what d'you say for yourself? You look at us and see nothing but air?" the tallest one among them gets himself off the upper bunk and starts out toward me.

The others follow him as if by command.

Scared as hell, I back away.

There are five of them.

Beanpole out front, closely followed by Oaf, the one who almost knocked me out, and the other three with equally bloodthirsty expression on their scar-distorted faces.

"Let's see what you've got in your satchel!" Beanpole swings the knife and grabs the handbag from the end of my bed. He practically rips open the zipper with his enormous paws and dumps the contents on the bed. He starts poking around in the pile with the tip of his knife.

"Where's your fag supply?" he hollers flashing the blade of his knife again. "Well, what's it going to be? Hey, pal?"

"Sorry, I'm all out," I no longer have a choice, I have to force myself to say something.

I can sense the quaking in my voice. My brain is drained of blood. I can say no more.

"What the hell! That all you can say, you cur? What were you thinking when you walked into the slammer without one lousy fag on you? Did ya imagine this was a welfare institution, a congregation of Benedictine nuns? Figure this was a fag factory? And look at this book! How come you didn't forget this bloody book? A jerk like you has no right to breathe the same air with us!"

Still sporting the knife, he turns to his companions. "What do you say, boys?"

They all find this hilarious.

They laugh with howls rattling the windows.

"Let's slit his throat!" Oaf hollers stepping up to his friend, trying to take possession of the knife.

"Not yet!" orders the other. "Take it easy, there's no hurry. Let's take our time and have a little fun." Beanpole shoves Oaf back in his place.

"He's got no fag, no pipe and didn't even bring a snack. You call this a man?" growls one of the other three.

"Why not finish him off, boys. Why screw around? Let's gag him and have a nice little bloodbath! Three days gone and no splish-splash!"

"But he didn't forget to bring his book" squeaks the shortest of the gang.

It seems to be a cue for Oaf to pounce on me, punching me in the face. I'm staggered, but it's not falling down I worry about but the nosebleed I feel developing. Soon it's dripping from my chin, on the floor. I unconsciously place my hand on my nose to pinch the nostrils shut.

The gang, all five of them, surround me, staring at the puddle of blood forming an inch from the tips of my shoes.

"All right, let's finish him off later," Beanpole turns around and strolls back to his bed in the corner.

The others follow him reluctantly.

"To the washroom, you pig!" bellows Oaf. "And if you breathe a word to the law out there you'll have your dick cut off."

As soon as I close the door behind me I find myself face to face with the sub-machinegun toting guard. He can see the blood on my hands and face, but he simply points to a door without a question.

In the washroom I carefully feel my nose with my fingertips. The slightest touch proves hideously painful.

Must be broken, I think while splashing cold water on it from the faucet. It's still dripping with blood. Not gushing like it did at first, but still dripping.

The blood mixed with water paints the sink a rose color.

I feel a presence behind me.

This time I decide there's no point in playing ostrich, and I turn around to face the inevitable.

The sub-machinegun cop is staring at me with an uneasy smile colored by pity.

"You know, everyone's got to go through this baptism by fire."

Back to the sink and my ablutions.

"Who did that to you? Beanpole?"

I shake my head.

"Then it must've been Oaf, the others only talk big."

I shake my head again.

"All right, I'm sure they threatened you with dire consequences. But I still need to know who did it."

More ablutions.

Silence behind me. For ten seconds. Then I hear steps receding. Before the door slams shut, I hear the sub-machinegun-toter. "Sooner or later I'll send them to hell!"

Slowly the bleeding subsides, only the pain persists. I find toilet paper in one of the cubicles and roll up a bunch, just in case the flow starts again. Take a last look at myself in the mirror before I venture out. My face is drained of color. In my eyes fear is gleaming. I close the washroom door behind me. I have no other choice but amble back to the so-called dormitory. Its door is only a few meters from the washroom. A number of possible scenarios flash through my mind. Should I return to my assigned place or ask the copper for help? I don't know why but I decide to return alone and face whatever lies ahead.

My hand is already on the door handle. Not too late to change my mind, I can't help telling myself, but by then the door is wide open. My legs carry me inside without my command, but I try to avert my eyes from the room and close the door with my eyes fixed on the more mundane features of my surroundings. Intent on avoiding any contact with my roommates I try to make my way to my bed with my eyes on the wall, but I end up bumping into Oaf. The whiteness of his nude body glistens like a ghost in the dim light.

I make an elaborate effort not to notice him by walking around him.

Before I reach my bed, I'm assaulted by a sudden burst of guffaws from behind; it sounds more like a pack of wolfs howling at the moon. I'm still afraid of looking behind me. Somehow I feel the bed offers a safe haven. There's no logical reason for this notion; the contents of my little brown bag lie scattered all over the blanket, and as I bend down to gather my possessions I'm hit by another volley of hoots and hollers from behind. This time I can't help looking in the direction of the renewed chorus. Oaf stands in the middle of the room rhythmically manipulating his solidly erect member.

"Jerk off, jerk off!" hollers Beanstalk, slightly rising from his bed for a better view.

The other three repeat the same phrase in a chorus.

"Jerk it off on his face! Let this cur have it!" commands Beanstalk getting up in order to push his minion toward me.

But he's too late; in the meantime, Oaf takes a step forward. And then another.

"Jerk off, jerk off, jerk off! On his dopy mug!" The four of them chant in devilish ecstasy.

Oaf keeps at it, rubbing his sex organ and turning toward me with a sneer. With every step he makes a pumping motion with his hips but without looking at me. He's totally engaged in the act of self-gratification.

"When you get it off shove it in his mouth!" one of the three minions puts in his penny.

"And cut his balls off," adds Beanstalk While tramping back to his bed. From under his pillow he pulls out the huge butcher knife and makes circles with it in the air, raising it high in a triumphant gesture. "With this, you see it?"

By then Oaf is standing by my bed. He speeds up the beat of his masturbation with his left hand while with the right he tries to trip me over the bed.

Suddenly, with a lot of clatter, the door flies open, and two policemen, armed with sub-machineguns, burst inside. Tense silence takes hold of the room.

"What is this sudden silence about?" one of them yells out casting his view around the room.

In a flash, Beanstalk slips the knife under the pillow, hardly making a move. Oaf, standing next to me, dives under my bed. He looks back at me from there with a finger on his lips; catching my eyes he uses the same finger to make like slitting his throat.

I'm frozen to the spot.

What am I to do?

The policemen stride to the middle of the dorm. They scrutinize my face.

"You all right?" one of them points a finger at me.

"Yes," I hear myself groan.

"Just set off the alarm if these gangsters try to harm you!" says the same cop wagging a finger at Beanstalk and his gang. "I swear I'll blast you guys to hell!" he goes on, and his tone of voice convinces me he means every word he says.

27

"No problem, boss," Beanstalk stretches out on his bed and, turning toward the Wall, he adds: "No one's going to suffer any harm."

The guardians of order are already on their way out. One of them slams the door behind them.

When quiet returns to the dorm Oaf crawls out fuming. He shakes a fist at me.

"You were lucky this time, you scumbag. Smart not to squeal." He spews the words at me on his way to retreat to the gang. His penis dangles harmlessly. His nude body wiggles across the floor like a pale apparition. His buddies greet him with renewed howls when he joins them.

"Things got pretty hot!" hollers one of them, giving the cue for the fiendish chorus of belly laughs.

For the time being I lie back on the cot, keeping an eye on Beanstalk and his gang. Waiting for the next assault. The minutes of abject fear go ticking at an excruciatingly slow rate. It seems to me time has stopped. I try to conjure up pleasant memories or images, but my mind goes blank as if all happy moments had sifted out of my life.

Oaf gets dressed again, and the others dig up a pack of cards from the night table. Soon the game is on.

"Get me some booze!" Beanstalk orders the fellow sitting across the table. The minion slowly sways his reptilian body off the chair and delivers a full bottle from a box under the bed. "Here you go," he grunts as he hands the bottle over to Oaf.

I keep listening to their disputes that accompany the game. I learn nothing to guide my future behavior towards them. Once in a while one of them gets unduly loud, but nothing else happens.

My eyelids keep shutting down. No, I must not fall asleep. If I do, they'll kill me, the thought nestles in my mind. I force myself to stay awake. But it's not easy. Some unseen, unknowable force keeps dragging me deeper and deeper below.

Above me the black bird of fear is circling.

In my dream I fall asleep and get stabbed in the heart.

* * * *

In a tunnel of light, I wander. Everything tangible escapes me. I'm standing in a malleable mixture of fog and light, or at least that is my impression; I believe I'm standing still even though the distance between me and the person I used to know as myself is steadily increasing. On the ballistic curve of dream-producing weightlessness I'm floating sometimes in uncontrollable plunge or soar up into ever-expanding space.

No question about it, I must be levitating, because I see nothing to get hold of, physical or conceptual; light, ideas, beliefs or aims are things I seek in vain. What's worse, I have no willpower to find my way out of this world of abracadabra-created sky and its trimmed puffs of cotton. On the other hand, there's nothing worse than the vain struggle of willpower in the absence of a way out.

I crawl and swirl in a whirlpool of winds without knowing if it's by my own effort or the environment. My soul, the focal point of my being, has floated off somewhere. I feel lonely and homeless in this new world and yet very much part of it; I have no thoughts or dreams of my own, they have mercifully vanished in the shifting shafts of light that crisscross the blank walls of my mere existence.

Like someone dead set on getting urgently undressed, liberating himself of coverings, divesting himself no matter what, I move along dropping items of clothing with elegant gestures on a garden path leading me away from the person I suspect of being myself. But I am also afraid of that someone; I'd like to take another look at his motionless, impassive face, but the distance between us is rapidly increasing. I'm wounded by the recognition that I'm no longer the man I used to think I was. But that man would not survive this suspended animation forced upon me.

All my senses have been plugged into a universal fog where my existence is indistinguishable from that of someone else next to me like waves in a light beam.

29

* * * *

"Screw it man, relax a little! Stretch out!" a voice growls at me from above, but I cannot look up, try as I can. And the voice goes on: "And what's this, screw it, man?"

I wish I could open my eyes at least to a slit, just enough to see the source of that voice. Instead, I clear my throat, but I can produce no more than a puny whine.

"Screw it, man, who the hell are you? Screw it..."

His words are dropping on me like sacks of sand.

The uneasy mixture of light and darkness begins to disperse. I'd like to stand up but can't make a move.

"What's all this blood, screw it?" The voce from above suddenly turns into a thunderclap.

Blood, blood, blood, the word echoes inside me. What blood? Where is it coming from?

Suddenly, without any effort on my part, my eyelids snap open.

The light is painfully cascading at me.

Blinding me.

Slowly the face bending over me takes shape. Thinning hair, bristly face and a luxuriant mustache under a wide nose.

"Screw it man, I thought you'd conked out, screw it. You gave me the willies, screw it."

Somehow the space between me and the mustache does not match the aggressively high volume of his voice, another source of pain. But the worst of it is in my left flank, just below the hip. When I reach out to touch the sore spot I find it wet.

They castrated me! The thought sends a jolt of horror through me, galvanizing me to action. I try to sit up and investigate the extent of my injuries.

"Someone stuck a knife into you!" Whiskers howls over me again, but now with less desperation and more like a statement of fact.

I look around the room. There are only the two of us, I and the trumpeter of the voice, the mustached young fellow.

30

What happened to me? I try to reconstruct the events of last night, but the only thing I come up with is the sad fact that they broke my nose.

I reach for my face.

There's indeed a spot in the middle of it that's sore to the touch, which, however, is no big deal in itself; it's a fact I can recall and observe even now, but what's happened since then? Where are my roommates, that gang I was forced by ill fate to share this living space with?

"Screw it, you were lucky, screw it. They hung it into your hip bone only, screw it."

"What?" I ask, confused by the word *hung*.

"Their switchblade, screw it, or knife. You got away with a wound, screw it."

"But where are they now? The other inmates?" I ask perfunctorily; curiosity is not exactly killing me. Not that I want to, but I should know if the others are sitting here with us and it's just that I cannot see them, or else they may have gone to the washroom for a cigarette or wherever.

"The others, screw it. What others? It's just us two in the room, screw it." Whiskers assures me.

"Hey you, Whiskers!" I cry out, and he quickly turns back to me.

"Screw it man, what's up, screw it?"

Drained of energy, I drop back flat on the bed.

What a strange character, what an exotic bird, I wonder lying helplessly. What on earth is he doing here? What chased him here? What force, purpose and determination flung him into this miserable story? Did he simply want to see the world? The future is unknown to us whichever side of the border we are on, so why exchange one unknown for another?

* * * *

"Now, you and I both agree you are an economic refugee, aren't you?" The interviewing official is a deceptively jovial looking, pudgy man, and his question keeps echoing in my

mind. It was something I had not expected. *What do you mean? What did you expect? Everyone who comes here has a purpose, a well-thought out goal. A goal. Don't you get it?* And you want me to confess to my goal? *Yes, that's the idea.* My goal, sir, I simply found myself on the run, helplessly and compulsively. *That's not a goal but an act.* Please let me explain. I came here out of fear. Yes sir, I was driven by fear. And still am. Fear has taken permanent residence inside me. Do you doubt that fear cannot be a premeditated, well-defined goal? The purpose of life, let's say. The way to self-realization. The sure and only path without any possible detours. And why not? You may ask. Because that path is the equivalent of the orbits followed by planets, determined by the law of mass attraction that also sets the distance between them. Similarly, everyone has a magnetic field that can attract either good or evil. Some people attract good mostly, others evil. I'd like to have your thoughts on the subject, but perhaps I should not irritate you with such superfluous ratiocination. Instead, I reduce the issue to this: my path is that of fear. It's this feeling that fires me up, drives me on and gives me strength to continue. Obviously, something that has not come to an end must continue.

No. I'm not asking you to agree with me.

In one word, it was fear that brought me here. *In that case you took refuge in the Regal for economic reasons?* The official gives me a piercing look. If fear is the same as economic reasons then yes, you're right, sir. *But what purpose did you have in mind coming here? We've clarified your reasons but not you purpose. Please address the question.* Sir, what purpose can a man have after fear has taken hold of him, filled him like concrete poured inside him and allowed to set in one overwhelming lump? *That's not the end of life. Don't tell me you eventually want to immigrate into a permanent state of fear?* In a way yes, from one state of fear to another. *You're impossible. In case you have not been aware of it, now let me make it clear to you that everyone must emigrate somewhere from the Regal. Whether by chance or choice, you have to end up on Continent A, B or C, in country X, Y or Z.* Do I have to decide now? *No, you'll have time for that after you get out of detention.* And when will that be? *As soon as we can check your identity.* And see who I really am? Am I the person I purport to be? *Exactly.* But can you also check who I will become? *What's that?* I repeat the question. *We're done for today. I'll have you taken back to the locked unit now.*

* * * *

"Screw it, man, I'm so hungry," Whiskers pokes me in the shoulder and sits down on the edge of the bed. "Screw it, you asleep? Screw it, you should have this cut stitched up, screw it, this cut is huge. You should call someone, screw it, your hip looks awful."

"Haven't got a bite to eat, sorry," I say with great effort; I feel very groggy, totally drained of all energy. "Please, go talk to the officer on duty."

"What do you want me to say, screw it, that I'm hungry, screw it?"

"Ask him to come here," I whimper weakly.

Next three characters in police uniform are rummaging under my blanket. They lift it off and raise the bloody thing, but I can't see it, lying as I am on my left side. They pull down my pants to the point previously investigated by Whiskers. The one guard within my limited field of vision has his submachinegun at the ready. And then he melts into light mixed with milky fog.

* * * *

"Let's call a doctor," suggests the policeman, who spreads the blanket over me again.

"Why? Can't he walk?" asks the other one.

"You saw him faint again just now," the first cop argues in a colorless tone.

By the afternoon I'm much better. The wound is cleaned, disinfected and sewn up.

"Screw it, you got three stitches," Whiskers mumbles when he sees me come awake.

I'm painfully hungry. Haven't eaten a thing since yesterday afternoon.

"Can you scrounge up a bite to eat?" I try to appeal to Whiskers sitting on the bed next to mine and picking at his fingernails. "I'm dying of starvation."

"Screw it, all I've got is a piece of bread. If you want it, screw it, I'll get it for you."

"Please, do," I nod though I'd like to run as far away from him as I could. I can't stand his language. Those *screw-it's* are getting on nerves.

"Here you go, screw it, I found a few slices of salami, too, screw it, maybe they haven't gone bad yet," says he, handing me a wrinkled white paper packet.

Slowly and gingerly I place my weight on my back. The cut in my hip is still aching, especially as I move, but once I settle down the pain abates. I break off a piece of the rye bread. It's dried out where it had been cut open and not sealed by the crust, but the saliva rushing into my mouth soon softens it to edible consistency. The salami smells, and it's not the smell of freshness. I sniff it several times to convince myself that it's only slightly over-aged but not quite rotten.

Whiskers watches me eat.

"Screw it, you sure didn't lose your appetite, screw it," he chuckles.

While eating I survey the room once more. There's no sign of the gang that attacked me last night. I wonder what happened while I was sleeping? They could have killed me. But why didn't they? My god, if they had slaughtered me, how free I'd feel already, the thought flashes through my mind. And I recall my dream in which they stabbed me in my heart.

I keep champing on the hard bread heel. Almost finished the whole thing. Of the salami only peels are left.

"May I ask you a favor?" I turn to Whiskers.

"Screw it, just say what you want, screw it."

"I wish you could cut back on the use of that *screw-it* phrase. It drives me out of my mind. I hope you don't take this little suggestion for an insult. Will you do me this favor?"

The wrinkles around his eyes smooth out as he assumes a serious expression. He seems to be doing some hard thinking.

"Screw it, I'll do it for your sake, screw it," he nods at me with his decision made, but then catches himself and shrugs his shoulders with a smile, with the merry little wrinkles rushing back to his eyes. "It's not gonna be easy for me to get used to it, but I'll give it a good try, screw it…"

* * * *

Later that afternoon, I learn from the guard making his usual rounds what happened last night after I'd fallen asleep. Oaf and his gang forced open the washroom window and lowered a rope to their confederates on the ground who attached a basket to it filled with cigarettes, drugs and a six-shooter. However, the guards on duty were watching the audacious operation, and they were the ones who emptied the basket in the washroom. They escorted my roommates in handcuffs to the more secure cells in the cellar. In the morning the creeps were turned over to criminal investigators.

But when did they stick the knife into me? The question doesn't let me rest. "Why didn't they simply kill me? They were playing with the idea, and could have carried it out.

Later I ask the same question from the guards, but they cannot come up with a satisfactory explanation either. "You're lucky to have got away with your life," one of them assures me in a tone of grim indifference.

His words leave a queasy echo in my mind. From his even, colorless tone of voice it's easy to deduce that he couldn't care less whether I got killed or not. Whiskers in the meantime has stretched out on his bed with his legs crossed and hands clasped on his chest. His whole ribcage is a wave, rising and falling.

Finally, I'm beginning to calm down. Through the window across the room the face of a red-haired, sad-eyed sky is peering in. The red tresses fly up in the air and spread out on the black iron bars.

For the first time in days I feel safe and secure. This may be a good time to start making plans for the immediate future, but I've run out of energy, both physically and mentally, and I totally surrender myself to the calm that settles over my heavy eyelids.

* * * *

The sound of an explosion rouses me again. The double door bursts open to inject a group of three guards. They're dragging a scruffy figure whose shabby attire speaks of a homeless man or a cave dweller in rags instead of animal skins. He's unsteady on his feet as if buffeted by wind or destabilized by narcotics. Maybe just drunk. The guards let him collapse on the nearest bed.

"Keep an eye on him, and report if his condition turns for the worse." One of the guards yells toward me and then shifts his gaze to Whiskers.

The latter is watching the proceedings in obvious shock. He too was roused from his dreams by the intruders. Neither of us says a word, as if by common consent. We just acknowledge the instructions with a nod and watch the departing guards with eyes still sticky from sleep.

The newcomer is lying on the bed in a fetal position. Whiskers slowly rises and approaches him, but finding the incidental light seeping in from outside too dim, he sweeps the wall with a hand for the switch. With the light on he returns to the rookie. He looks him over and finally pokes him with his hand.

"Screw it man, are you okay?"

A whimper detaches itself from the motionless figure and drags itself across the room.

"Screw it, this guy's had it, screw..." he stops himself in his tracks when he turns to me as if for confirmation. "Looks like to me he's about to conk out."

The newcomer responds by slowly sitting up at the edge of the bed with his feet on the floor, but then his torso falls forward. Whiskers sits down on a bed across and bends down to find eye contact with the captive.

"How about water, screw it?" he repeats the question two more times.

"Yeah," whispers the other and raises his head.

It's hard to tell if his face is covered with a beard or mud or both. His long, neglected hair curtains his eyes, but still he doesn't look much older than twenty, still a mere lad.

Whiskers in the meantime goes out and returns with a plastic jar in hand.

When he hands it over some of the water slops on the floor.

"The best I could do, screw... you know we got no glasses here," he looks at me apologetically.

The Lad raises the jar to his lips with shaking hands. Takes a sip and then downs the whole jar without stopping for a breath.

Whiskers stays standing next to him, keeping an eye on him. Then relieves him of the empty jar.

"I hope you fellows don't mind if I lie down now, I'm exhausted," says Lad in a faint voice and drops back on the bed.

Silence returns to the night. Whiskers switches off the light.

"Screw it, I first thought they delivered a cadaver here," he remarks with a deep sigh and ambles back to his bed.

For the longest time I cannot go back to sleep.

With a pounding heart I feel long, sharp minutes press their way through my body.

* * * *

"Hello, fellow inmates! Mathematician is my profession, but my specialty is computer programming," with this exuberant announcement an athletic, tall young man hoists a huge suitcase on the bed next to mine. When he realizes he woke me up he continues in a more normal tone of voice. "Sorry, I just arrived with the early express train. Just as expected we were stranded at the border, surrounded by customs coppers. They were looking for contraband, but lo and behold, I was a few steps ahead of them," he snorts-laughs at his humor and pulls a folded document from the lining of his attaché case. "My good fellows, look at this, my engineering diploma, the original document!" he waves the papers over his head and then he refocuses on me. "In a word, I'm right on track. What an experience, a pleasure trip into freedom! From here I'll be flying to the exact opposite point on Earth. My fiancée is waiting for me. Well, kiddos, I'm finally here!" he goes on with great flair as if declaiming from a stage, a special one that has the whole world revolving around it.

He snaps open his suitcase, takes out pajamas and from a plastic bag toothbrush and toothpaste. He heads for the door with confident strides.

Whiskers has a befuddled expression as he keeps switching his gaze from Mathman to me with a bewildered expression.

I still wonder about the newcomer of last night. I see a pile of blankets on his bed and assume he's still asleep underneath.

"I don't get it, screw it," Whiskers turns to me after Mathman slams the door behind him, "putting on airs, isn't he? This condescending behavior, screw it, what's that about? Why is he trying to put everybody down? What's he trying to say? What's the big deal? While some people arrive by express train, screw it, others flee across the minefield risking their lives, like that Lad, screw it?"

Now it's my turn to look befuddled.

"Where did you get that story?"

Whiskers holds back answering my question. He stares at the wall as if he had to rummage through a large stack of memory files in order to find the latest one. Waiting patiently, I refrain from hindering him in his work.

"I woke up in the middle of the night and I saw Lad too was awake. Just sitting on his bed, staring at the floor. I offered assistance, but he didn't want anything. Not even water. So I just sat with him in silence, and after a while he started to speak, telling me his life's story. He grew up in a village close to the border. He finished eight years of primary school but just barely; book learning was not his strong point and he preferred the company of shepherds. He was nineteen when there was a case of missing lambs and lamb chops appearing on the produce market. He was arrested for the suspicion of theft. At the trial he was convicted to half a year in jail even though the judge suspected that the shepherds had butchered the lambs, but three of them testified under oath against Lad. In jail he was subjected to unnatural sexual acts, and by the time he got out he was a sex worker for men. He moved to a nearby large city and made living using his newly acquired 'trade'. One day he received a letter from home with another letter inside. It was from the States from a cousin who made good in the New World and now it was Lad's turn to run across the border. If he made it, the cousin promised in the letter to take care of him and make arrangements for Lad to join him in the States. He read the letter several times. Then he took the bus to his village that very night and headed for the border on a trail he knew well from his childhood. What he didn't know was that in the meantime they had placed landmines along the border. At the sound of the first explosion he started running like crazy. His run stirred up such fireworks that even on the other side they declared emergency. They thought it was a wild boar that had set off the sound and light show, but when they saw a human figure emerge from the reddish fog, the soldiers on both sides turned silent. Maybe they were all rooting for the crazy hurdle runner to make it across in one piece." At this point Whiskers falls silent although it's clear he has more to say.

"And you know what? No harm came to our hero..." Mathman finishes the story for Whiskers in a sneering tone while drying his enormous paws with a tiny towel. There is a smug expression on his face, a sure sign of more one-upmanship to come.

"Don't you realize I heard the poor fugitive say he's hoping to move on to the States? We know it's out of the question; they don't allow anyone with a prison record to enter that country. He'd better find that out now from me rather than an unsympathetic stranger." He lets his gaze move from one to another of his roommates and bursts out into guffaws. He's definitely enjoying the crude fun he's having at our expense.

I can't help telling him not to bother in our behalf, leave us to our blessed ignorance. We have no need of helpful information, but...

"Go jump into a lake, screw it!" Whiskers turns demonstratively the other way.

Mathman pretends not to hear. He bends down to reach his suitcase under the bed and packs away his toiletry articles.

He's caught on his knees when the door flies open with a racket as if it had been kicked down by the uniform coming in. The sub-machinegun is casually slung in his shoulder. His relaxed body language speaks of exaggerated self-confidence. He stands there projecting the image of a man who has nothing and no one to fear, but he expects everyone to fear him.

"In five minutes I'll be taking you guys to breakfast," his gaze takes in all of us, one by one, and then he adds in a louder, more commanding tone: "Right after that, the interrogations will commence."

The representatives of authority all over the world speak so curtly, arrogantly, and one might add, without any common courtesy due to all fellow human beings; I weigh the situation in my mind and discover I'm slowly losing that sense of fear I came in with.

"Interrogation?" Whiskers sounds surprised once we are alone again.

"What an imbecile!" Mathman snaps at him immediately. "When they brought you in, didn't they tell you they were going to question you?"

"I've been questioned already," says Lad.

40

"Well, screw it, that doesn't surprise me. Considering the circumstances, screw it, the way they brought you in..." Whiskers stares at him.

"Okay, so they'll question me again... I have nothing else to say except what I said before..." Lad shrugs it off.

"They're looking for spies from the great proletarian empire," Mathman raises a forefinger. "Be on your guard, watch your tongue! They loathe economic refugees; they consider them spies. Watch every word you say. If they ask you whether you're an economic refugee answer NO! at once. Don't hesitate for a second. Remember what to say: I am not an economic refugee! I escaped to the Free World out of political conviction. I hate the dictatorship of the proletariat and its religion! I seek political asylum! Capisce? You got that?" Mathman bears down on us with big eyes popping out of his red face.

* * * *

The door opens. The same cop appears. He gives us a contemptuous, haughty look.

He can't see what we see.

He can't feel what we feel.

He can't think what we think.

He's power personified.

He says nothing, and we stand around without a clue, with eyes on him. Or maybe on nothing.

"Fall into single file!" he commands like a sergeant and opens the door.

Mathman is to lead the way and we fall in behind him.

All three of us.

I limp. My hip hurts with every step.

The electric lock buzzes on the door.

We're out in the stairway.

The gunshot riddled window shocks me more than yesterday. The bloodstains seem to have a more vivid hue.

41

Getting through a second door we continue our way in a corridor. Our armed guard walks next to us, seemingly paying no attention to his charges. After a corner he stops us and steps forward to unlock the door with an old-fashioned key. We enter a huge mess hall, partitioned off by glass walls.

Rows of long tables and benches along them fill the space in this great hall that was obviously designed with its function in mind with military—almost brutal—simplicity. I can just imagine classes of cadets marching in and lining up at the assigned tables and standing at attention while they recite a brief prayer until the order is barked out to sit. Come to think of it, not much difference between military barracks and prisons,

We are directed to a cafeteria counter where a kind faced, pudgy lady ladles out the food into aluminum soup bowls and fills aluminum mugs with tea. With quick, well-practiced movements.

Within minutes we're seated at a table in silence and spooning in what appears to be a meat and potato stew. I take big bites of the fresh bread, and before I notice my bowl is empty.

The others are taking their time with the meal.

I wait for them sipping my tea. And thinking about the cozy restaurant where I had lunch with my aunt just before she dropped me off at the Regal.

* * * *

The building is old, which lends some verisimilitude to the rustic décor of the restaurant. One might call it an inn. The menu is not extensive. Nor pretentious. Just plain country dishes. Finally, we settle on venison in sweet and sour sauce with *knedl*, dumplings spiked with croutons, because they come from the refrigerator and could be served in short order according to the waiter.

42

I can still taste venison and the current jelly served on a leaf of bib lettuce. We wash down the luxurious meal with new red wine of the fall.

The gourmet lunch is somewhat marred by the thought of moving into the Regal directly from the table. My aunt doesn't seem to be bothered by this minor detail. I fail to detect the slightest shadow of apprehension on her face. She's totally engaged in the task of cutting the meat into bite-size pieces and then bathing them in the sauce. I am alone with the thought that I am on the most pivotal threshold of my life. She concentrates on the venison and the dumpling, sparing me only a few stray glances. No wonder; our acquaintance is of very fresh origin, and it is not to last very long.

* * * *

Here I am, sitting in the mess hall and sipping my tea, waiting for the others to finish their breakfast. The story of my meeting my aunt seems far removed from my present circumstances, opaque to the point of unreal. Something that didn't happen to me but a fictional character I'd read about in a book. The steam from the tea condenses on my face, collecting into one big, very labile drip on the tip of my nose. It sends a jolt through my whole body. Another reason for self-pity and a feeling of incompetence. All my strength has abandoned me. While watching the others exercise their jaws, I remember our next appointment with destiny, the interrogation.

According to Mathman, I'll have to deny I am an economic refugee. The thought is intriguing: if I cannot define freedom, if I cannot verbalize the meaning of the Free World in concrete terms, how can I possibly dispute being labeled an economic refugee.

Mathman has an easy answer to that: anyone who hates communism cannot be an economic refugee, by definition. That's the key, the very solution to the problem.

The magic word that will open the gate to success.

Salesmanship. Mathman waltzed into Austria with a passport. How was he politically repressed? If he can claim political status, anyone can. It's a question of how you sell yourself.

The guard who'd taken charge of us is sitting in a corner, cradling the sub-machinegun in his lap. He's not engaged in any activity, physical or mental. The guardian of power happens to be bored.

Whiskers is the second to finish breakfast, followed by Mathman and Lad.

Climbing the steps. Four destinies, four hopes, four indescribable anxieties are marching back to the holding pen.

On the first landing my injury suddenly acts up. A jolting pain that gradually gives way to numbness. Maybe I wouldn't even pay attention to it except for the fact that at the same time I'm overtaken by a feeling of sadness and undefined longing. It must be that bodily pain is the manifestation of the soul.

For the second day I hear nothing from my family. The last time I talked to my wife I told her only what I felt would help preserve her peace of mind. It was not an easy job to perform. How can a husband restore his wife's serenity after his unexpected departure, leaving her alone with their two children? That sudden change is hard to bear if the husband has to live in the next town. How much harder if he is –having committed the serious crime of illegal border crossing – living in another world, separated by historical forces beyond the control of ordinary mortals? The voices of my two little boys came to me only to the extent of a hurried greeting on the telephone. In my mouth the sour taste of separation and despondency, before me the challenge of solving an existential mathematical equation with several unknowns:

1. Will I be successful in obtaining an immigration permit to one of the countries of the Free World?
2. Will I be able there to stand on my own feet, find a job and forge a new future?

3. Will I manage to have my family join me there before my absence can estrange me from them and they get used to life without me?

I'm clambering up the steps like on a rocky mountainside. Our armed guard escorts us back to our room, but then he returns in the next minute. He calls out Mathman's name. He's the one to be interrogated first.

While he's out the rest of us make our beds, take care of our meager possession and thoughts. No matter how hard I try to convince myself I have nothing to worry about, my stomach feels tied up in knots.

The doubts, worries and imponderables defy verbal definition: that's why they keep swirling uncontrollably in my mind.

"Hurray, fellows, it's all set, I'm flying to Australia!" Mathman bursts in on us. His face is beaming with happiness as if he were already on the plane.

The process went smoothly, without a hitch. The 'pencil pusher' – as he calls the official in charge – is eager to get on, but not a bad sort. He's between retirement and the grave, and he just follows the routine," he keeps repeating as if to convince himself. "Let me warn you again, don't even give the slightest hint that you may be economic refugees. Deny it at all costs if he tries to brand you with that." Ambling toward his cot, the engineer can't stop talking. "One other thing. As I mentioned before, they're sniffing for spies. Watch what you say, the old geezer can turn every word around and give it a different meaning. Don't open your mouth except to answer a question. And then choose your words carefully, making the answer simple, straightforward, and to the point. No rambling, no qualifying phrases, no 'but...' no 'the way I feel...' definitely no 'it occurred to me...' no 'in my opinion...'"

Whiskers is toying with a mysterious smile as if in possession of an insider betting tip.

Lad seems preoccupied with his own thoughts without paying attention to the room.

45

I take Mathman's warnings with a grain of salt.

"You're next," the engineer targets Lad with his forefinger. "You'll have a lot to talk about."

As soon as Lad slams the door behind him Mathman resumes his triumphant report:

"My god, you should've seen the old weasel's face when I produced my original engineering certificate!"

"Come on, screw it, you really think the weasel gives a shit whether you have a diploma or not?" Whiskers snaps back from his bed. "You can wipe your ass with it, screw it! You think you're so important, screw it? The hell you are. You're just one number on a long list of numbers, a statistical entry, screw it, an entry they can twist around according to their needs. What's the big deal about that piece of paper, screw it? You think you're the only one who knows how to matriculate, screw it? Anyone can do it..."

Mathman's eyes are on fire. He's about to launch a counter attack, he opens his mouth but then dismisses Whiskers with a contemptuous wave of his hand and a condescending glance. He turns around, bends down to retrieve his suitcase and place it on top of the bed. He rummages in one corner and then another, pulling his hand out with disappointment until sudden his face betrays he has in his hands what he's been looking for.

From a wax paper package a long piece of salami rolls out. He cuts thick slices with a pocketknife.

After a while he notices Whiskers's hungry stare. Visibly embarrassed, he holds out the slices on their wax paper tray toward us.

Whiskers demonstratively turns away in a huff, I shake my head with a grateful smile. And yet I am almost visibly salivating. The recently consumed breakfast left no impact in my stomach. I'm hungry as hell, and lunchtime is far off in the future.

The armed guard said we had the last seating in the mess hall; those in the holding pen are not allowed to mingle with the general population of the camp. By the rules and regulations of the Regal. Declining Mathman's invitation to

46

join him in the feast doubles my hunger pains. I can't keep my eyes off the salami.

"Listen," says the engineer to the room with food in his mouth, "you can be a good boy here but never clever enough. I came here well-prepared with the benefit of the earlier escapees' experiences. All the info they had to offer. It'll come in handy now. My one goal is to get to Australia as soon as possible. My fiancée is a Wonder Woman. She works at a real estate agency. She's lined up a job for me already in a computer store where they do hardware repair work as well as smaller programming. We are planning to buy a house in a nice quiet neighborhood where the kids can grow up in peace, and..."

"Screw it man," Whiskers cuts him off, "Who the hell wants to know all about your plans? That's your business. You can talk all you want, screw it, but nobody's listening to your long, boring spiel, screw it!"

"I only wanted to help. But if you find my well-meant advice offensive, I didn't say a word. Agreed?" Mathman takes a big bite out of his salami.

* * * *

The door clanks open. Lad enters with head hanging low. Without looking left or right, he makes directly for his cot.

We follow him with our eyes.

It shows on him he's in some kind of a trouble. Obviously, the interview didn't go in his favor.

Whiskers is all nerves, he keeps shifting his gaze from Lad to Mathman and me, and then back to Lad.

"Tell us, screw it, what happened?" His voice is hoarse.

"You're next, they're waiting for you in the office at the other end of the corridor," Lad says to Whiskers without raising his head.

"So here it goes, it's my turn, screw it," Whiskers leaps to his feet giving Mathman a dirty look. "This stuff about

47

economic refugees, screw it, is it true?" he asks Lad on his way out but doesn't receive an answer.

Curiosity is killing me. What happened to Lad? What got him down so much? I go to him and sit down on the edge of his cot.

"Tell us all about it. What happened?" I get hold of his arm, but in a moment I let go.

"Sooner or later they're going to send me home," he answers softly. "Mathman was right; no country will have me on account of my prison record. And I'm not going to stay here," he points a finger at the floor. "It's my choice. They're giving me a little time to think it over. So that's it. And I was all set to go to the States."

"If they're giving you time to make up your mind, you still have a chance. Maybe you can go to Australia," I reason, but I find the idea ludicrous. Immigration rules and regulations don't change that easily. But I can't stop encouraging him. "At one time Australia was a place where they sent convicts, so don't lose hope…"

"Why would I go there? I don't know a soul there," Lad shakes his head. "I want to join my cousin. And he's the States. With him around I would not be alone in the world. Loneliness kills me. Often I got in trouble only because I was trying to make friends with someone. Everything I try turns against me."

I'm lying on my cot. Looking at the fly-flecked ceiling. There's a stabbing pain in my hip area. Suddenly my one place of rest becomes uncomfortable.

I'm tense and restless. I'm next. I'm going to be interrogated, and I'm dumbstruck; tension grips my throat, and my hands are shaking to a restless rhythm. I attempt to take refuge in joyous memories. Faint sunshine flashes across the sky.

This is the best of all possible worlds, and it's up to me to adapt my spirit to it. It's not impossible, it's a matter of willpower, I assure myself.

"They could do something about this screwed up door, screw it," Whiskers, obviously irritated by the explosive noise the door makes, remarks as he steps in the room and then turns to Mathman: "It's all set, screw it, you know-it-all. Now it's your turn, screw it," he adds leisurely, waving at me. He sits down with Lad.

Stepping out to the corridor I run into the armed guard. He points to a door at the end of the corridor.

In the office I find a somewhat corpulent sixtyish man behind a desk. He merely grunts in answer to my proper greeting. He's busy riffling through his file folders.

"They neglected to take your fingerprints," he says with annoyance. "That's what I'm looking for without any success."

I remain silent, not recalling that particular procedure.

"That's all right, they'll take care of it when we get done here," he sighs waving me to a chair on the other side the desk.

He feeds a blank sheet into the typewriter. Actually three sheets with two carbon papers between them.

He types fast and at an even speed.

Says my name, birthplace and date.

I nod to each bit of data.

He names the spot where I entered the country.

This time I answer with a *yes*.

Without looking at me he continues typing for a while, stopping suddenly to lean back in his swivel chair. With his two hands on the back of his head he closes his eyes.

"All right. Now tell me your story. What prompted this little excursion?" he sneers at the word 'excursion'.

He has his eyes on me.

My hands are lying in my lap, the fingertips mechanically circling one another. My sweaty palm makes me nervous. I cannot find the right words.

"Please, go ahead. I'm all ears," he prods me again.

At first, I am full of circumlocution. At least that's how it seems to me. I tell all that happened before my escape. I speak about my plans going wrong, about my coworkers' attitude toward me, and why I failed in my journey of self-discovery. I ended my recitation with a rather detailed report on the night I spent in the cellar of the State Security Agency.

"Did they beat you?"

"They tried, but I dodged the blow."

"Did they threaten you?"

"Likely, yes."

"Yes or no?"

"That's how it seemed to me."

"What were you afraid of?"

"I don't know. It was a new experience for me, something strange. I could not get that fear out of my mind."

"That's not enough. You know how many people in the Soviet Empire have been beaten up and threatened with death?"

I have no answer.

"Not counting all the people, they tortured in their prisons for years. Compared to that, what happened to you is a trifle, nothing. So what was the real reason for your escape?" he looks at me like a strict teacher talking to a truant.

"Fear. I was afraid."

"Afraid? Of what?"

"I don't really know."

Can't these people understand that fear is in the very fabric of a dictatorial society? Everybody lives in fear. Those who have been threatened, and those who have not, because it might come any day, and they must do everything to stave it off. Try to explain that to a corpulent bureaucrat in the Free World.

"Did you eventually sign a confession?"

"No."

"Are you sure?"

"Yes."

"Why didn't you if I may ask?"

"Because..."

"If you don't tell the truth, sooner or later we'll find out exactly what happened. In effect, you are an economic refugee?"

50

Hearing that loaded question I get frazzled. I take a deep breath, trying to overcome my nervousness.

"If this is your conclusion from all that I told you, then perhaps you're right, I am." I surrender in the hope of cutting the whole thing short.

And then the warning Mathman kept repeating comes back to me. Too late to backpedal now. I'm at my wit's end.

"Sonny boy, when you fellows come here you all try to play the persecuted political victim, and then it turns out you were all motivated by economic reasons for the escape. This is obvious to me from what you've told me. You tried to open a seltzer bottling plant, grow mushrooms on commercial scale, and when none of these ventures came to fruition, you simply took to your heels. You thought you'd be successful in the Free World. That's not how it works, my son. Life is not all peaches and cream here either. You'll find out for yourself soon enough."

I don't make a move in my chair. The tension paralyzes me, but I watch intently. All at once my interrogator recovers the use of his hands and starts typing at his fast, even pace. When the page is all filled up he pulls it out with one swing of his hand and feeds new sheets of paper in place of the old. He repeats this performance once more.

"The US, Canada or Australia, these are your choices. You have to emigrate to one of these countries, you are not to stay here," raising his face from the papers he gives his verdict and pushes a sheet of paper with only a few lines typed on it. "Sign it on the dotted line. It says you acknowledge that you are in this country only temporarily and must move on."

I sign it without reading the statement.

Then he separates the pages from the carbon sheets. He places the three-page document before me. Pokes a finger to the spot where I have to sign it.

"May I read it?" I look at him.

"No need for you to read it," he snaps at me. "It only says what you just related to me."

My eyes land on the first page. I scan the top part quickly. Name, birthplace, date of birth, and the status: political escapee.

My hand no longer shakes when I sign it.

"And now go to the office at the other end of this corridor to get fingerprinted," he commands gruffly, and returns my goodbye with another grunt.

* * * *

The black ink drop spreads out on the marble surface. A rubber roller goes over the spot, and it's hard to see where the ink drop vanished. Each fingertip of mine leaves its print on a lined cardboard.

"All done," says the officer wiping his hand in a rag. "You can wash your hands clean with soap and bicarbonate there, in the sink," he points to the corner of the large hall and returns his attention to the tools of his trade.

I return to my room.

Tense silence fills the place.

I can feel the gaze of my roommates on the back of my head.

None of them speaks up. They're waiting for me to give a full report on the interview. But I don't feel like talking. I'm hungry.

It's well past noon, it's time for them to take us to lunch. I lie flat on my back. My hip hurts again. Before my closed eyes the events of the last hour play themselves out like a film. It was a lucky thing I didn't say one word about old Blackteeth. I can still see his ruddy face and smell his garlicky breath. It was only a little over a hundred hours ago when the car turned back with him and left me standing in a cloudburst adorned with lightning bolts.

Alone.

"Well, what status did you earn?" Mathman asks casually while fiddling with his hand bag.

"Political," say I, almost as if speaking to myself.

"You were just trying to scare us, screw it, with that economic nonsense, screw it," Whiskers raised his voice gradually. "I'm sure both of you got the political status."

"Not me!" Mathman growled. "Not me!"

"You don't deserve it either," cuts in Lad, looking at us as if surprised by what he's saying against his will. "You just got on the train, and…" He shuts up, noticing the sparks of hatred in Mathman's eyes.

Who knows what the tension could have led to if the armed guard had not marched in with: "Lunch time. Fall in line."

I stuff myself silly thanks to Mathman who shares the second course with me. "I ate so much salami, I lost my appetite," he pushes his aluminum plate toward me before he tastes it. At the end though he doesn't touch the remaining half but gives it to Lad.

The afternoon is quiet on the third floor.

The interviews are over.

The residents of the adjacent rooms don't make a sound either. I'm dying of curiosity but too afraid to venture among strangers. I have enough tension to put up with right here, no need to go looking for it elsewhere.

The interview depleted us of all energy.

After lunch discussion already focuses on possibilities after our release from the holding pen.

Mathman is again way ahead of us. He's got a temporary job lined up already. And not just menial work; he's going to get a ride to a nearby mansion where he'll be assisting in the installation of a new telecommunication system.

The paramedic wakes me up. He's here to change the bandages on my wound. The antiseptic cream stings a little. He says in two days he'll take out the stitches. Till then I'll have to keep water out of it. I ask him to take a look at my nose since he's here already, but please do it gingerly.

He produces a pliers-like tool from his bag. It hurts like hell when he applies it to my nose.

"Yes indeed, it's broke all right," he says swaying his head from side to side. He gives the Latin name of the bones involved.

"It'll heal in a week. But to restore it would require surgery," he remarks before leaving.

At dinner the guard on duty tells me Oaf was shot trying to escape that afternoon. One bullet burrowed into his left leg and the other in one of his elbows.

Mathman and Whiskers are also there to hear the story. They don't show any interest in who Oaf might be. They simply acknowledge the fact that someone they don't know got shot as if it were a mundane, everyday event.

Whiskers even comments: "Good name, Oaf, screw it."

Milky White fog swirls with the lights, mesmerizing me.

I let it. I'm fog.

* * * *

Quiet evening. Mathman is rummaging in his suitcase placed on the bed. He picks up an item almost randomly and holds it up to his eyes for closer scrutiny as if not quite trusting his sight. He subjects the corkscrew set to thorough examination, opens the blade like pocketknife, closes it again and buries it at the bottom of the suitcase. Whiskers is laid back on his bed, still dressed and with shoes on. His eyes are fixed on the ceiling. His look betrays his thoughts are far off somewhere else.

Lad has just left the room.

It's the first time in quite a while that I feel safe. It's an interesting thought: safety is something I'll have to get used to; I've been living in uncertainty and danger much too long. Back home, and here too. The change is unexpected, I'm not ready for it. Yet one should prepare oneself for desired eventualities as well as the undesired ones.

Somehow I'll manage to graduate from this institution, I assure myself.

A few days after the interview most escapees are let out of detention, allowed to go free in and out of the Regal, says the armed guard that afternoon. Although his voice is tainted with antipathy, the sound of the word "free", I know, will forever tinkle sweetly in my ears as the harbinger of real freedom and the hope of taking a walk in the park next just outside of the Regal.

I long to be among trees.

I wake to Whiskers shaking my shoulder.

"Come, Mathman wants to offer you salami. They tell him he's getting out tomorrow, he's got no reason to hoard food."

The eatables are spread out on a newspaper. We sit in a circle around Mathman's bed, picking up the remains of his pantry.

It has turned dark outside.

Two or three lights, skewered on lamp posts, emerge from the night like stray lightning bugs.

* * * *

Next afternoon a fiftyish man in civilian clothes walks into the room accompanied by two armed guards. The word gets stuck in Mathman's throat; he happens to be lecturing us on the virtues of Australia.

"Good afternoon!" announces the official-looking man heading for the middle of the room. The guards follow him without bothering with greeting us. They seem to be sizing us up.

One of them hands an open note book to the civilian. He reads off a list of our names and tucks the note book under an arm. For a few long seconds he scrutinizes our faces. All four of us stand by our cot, frozen to the spot. We don't know what to make of the late afternoon visitor.

"You people will be leaving here tomorrow morning," says the man still scanning our faces. "You will bundle up your bed linen and drop them off in the ground-floor stockroom where you got them a few days ago. Next, you will present yourselves in the registration office located in the yellow building in the right corner of the quadrangle. The first order of business is getting a Regal card. I warn you," he stops here for dramatic effect, "getting the card is of utmost importance. Without the card you cannot walk through the gate, neither in, nor out. Without the card you cannot proceed with your further business. The card is your I.D. within the borders of this country."

He takes a break again, still watching us. His gaze keeps returning to Whiskers.

"That's all I have to say. You'll be informed of the details tomorrow," he adds after turning around to leave. But he turns back yet again from the door. "In the registration office you'll be told you cannot stay in this country. So don't even try. Instead, you should be making every effort to move on, the sooner the better. You did not escape just to be a refugee forever. Good night," he gives a slight nod and marches out of the room, accompanied by the armed guards.

The door slams with its usual loud bang behind them.

For a few seconds we remain standing like stone monuments.

"Hurray, screw it, tomorrow we'll be free, screw it!" yells out Whiskers.

His eyes are glistening.

He walks over to Lad sitting on his bed, his eyes lost in nothingness.

"Come on, away with that hangdog look, screw it! Who knows, maybe you'll make it to the States," Whiskers pokes Lad in the ribs.

Mathman starts whistling a cheerful ditty. He pulls his suitcase from below his bed and starts sorting through its contents.

"Who's ready for salami? Look, you fellows, look how much we still have left. We have to finish the whole thing!" He invites us to the little table quickly conjures up. He cuts thick slices, eager to get to the end of the long salami roll.

Whiskers takes big bites, gesturing to Lad to join in the feast. I pick up a slice from the paper and nibble on it. Somehow I've lost my appetite. And yet I suffer hunger pains all the time. Now that I know I'll be free tomorrow, suddenly I don't know what to do with myself. The torturing sensation of fear has suddenly ceased, as if a glowing hot iron rod had been pulled out of my chest; I no longer feel any pain, even the wound has healed all of a sudden. In place of fear an inexplicable desire has settled, stirring up restlessness inside me, a vague but weighty desire that whips up my nerves and fills me with jitters. It soon outgrows its nest, overwhelms me. At the same time, I feel the lack of something, as if I had lost something essential, something that once enriched my life with meaning and purpose, promising willpower and readiness to fight.

I step up to the window.

The realization hits me: I never once looked outside all the time I've been here. The numbness of being tied into knots by fear has prevented me from ever looking beyond the walls.

The setting sun paints pink the puffy clouds gathering on the horizon.

The slipping sky hangs on to the foliage of the trees standing on guard around the yard.

Eternity may be like this, I think with my forehead on the cool window pane. Expecting a miracle, I stay like this looking at the landscape frozen into its essence. The foliage stays still.

No wind tousles their leafy hair.

* * * *

It takes me forever for me to fall asleep. I have to go home first. I unlock the front gate with a clumsy, old-fashioned key. It's past eleven, quite late, everyone in my family is asleep. I tiptoe into the entrance foyer and take my coat off. Turn the light on, wash my hands in the bathroom, open the refrigerator and collect slices of cheese and ham. I automatically reach into the cabinet for bread. Sure enough, it's there waiting for me in

57

its basket, wrapped in a linen serviette. I cut two slices, replace the remaining portion in the serviette and put it back in its place. Next, I want to spread butter on the slices, but then I realize I forgot to get it from the fridge. So I open it again and find the butter.

I see my hands spreading butter on bread. Then come the cheese and ham. I take a healthy bite out of the sandwich.

The bedroom door opens.

My wife appears in the opening, rubbing sleep out of her eyes.

"Why so late coming home again?" she asks sitting down on the green-painted kitchen stool. She pulls the bathrobe tighter on her chest.

"You cold?" I'm concerned.

She smiles.

"The boys asleep yet?"

"Yes, today granny took them to the daycare center. They called me in to work. At eight-thirty, they said the state security people wanted to have a chat with me immediately."

"Why at work?"

"That's what I asked, too, why not come here like before?"

"What did they want?"

"The same old rigmarole; who are your friends, do I know them, where do you go after work, what have you been up to..."

"As if they didn't know already. They're always on my track. This afternoon when I came out of the office building, there were two of them tailing me. One of them ambling on one side and the other on the opposite side. Today they came up with a new twist to their act. One of them was laughing like a horse when he told me what a dumb creature I was, didn't I know you've had a lover for the past few months."

"And what did you say?"

"I said yes, I know."

"And what then?"

"No and. They stared at me with their stupid look and laughed. My god, how disgusting they can be."

58

"Their latest campaign is all about ruining your reputation; one of my coworkers warned me."

I don't feel like eating any longer. I put down the sandwich I started only minutes before.

"Come, let's go to sleep. I'm going to have a hard day tomorrow."

No matter how carefully we pick our steps in the room, the floorboards crack now and then. Not too loudly, but enough to disturb us even if not the kids.

The two boys are sleeping side by side in one bed. The younger one has a thumb in his mouth. I peel off my clothes as quietly as I can. I lie down, close my eyes. It takes forever for me to fall asleep.

* * * *

I'd love to leap out of bed like Whiskers, but when I turn over the pain comes as a jolt into my hip, and I can feel a grimace gripping my face.

Whiskers catches a glimpse of it.

"You have to exercise, screw it, because in the Free World, screw it, you can go, screw it, where you want. You'll make a pretty sight, screw it, if the first day you can't make a move. What's going to happen to you later, screw it?" he says it loudly, more like to the room, he doesn't even look at me.

Mathman tells Lad to hurry up, get himself organized; we have to drop off the bed linen and he isn't even dressed yet.

Barely finished getting ready to check out when an armed guard walks into our room.

"I have to escort you jailbirds, you ready?" he asks with the contemptuous grin that seems to be part of his uniform. Then he looks at Lad still standing undecided with one sheet in his hand. "Don't leave anything behind!"

Whiskers swings his bundle over his shoulder, Mathman drags his still heavy suitcase behind him and I have my little brown bag.

We nod to the guard, ready to go.

The lock clanks.

Soon our steps are echoed in the ground floor corridor. In the stockroom a fortyish, balding man stands behind the low counter. Our guard gives him a list. One by one we hand over the dirty linen.

The door opens and we leave the premises without saying goodbye. We trudge in the tracks of the armed one.

We find ourselves outside in the four-sided courtyard.

The fresh morning air feels good. It seems to have some flower scent mixed into it by the breeze.

That's just my imagination playing a trick on my nose; autumn is upon us, where would flowers come from this time of the year? I argue with myself.

No rush, just a slow march.

Mathman complains: couldn't we walk a little slower, his suitcase is damn heavy.

The other sides of the quadrangle are made up of one- and two-story buildings; these wings of the central building were to meant as service quarter to the academy, perhaps even stables and carriage houses and later expanded into administrative offices.

I catch sight of that crucial yellow structure. We're headed in its direction, following a line of trees.

Soon we're in the lobby of the Registration Center. Our guard steps into one of the offices. He closes the door behind him. After a few minutes of standing we get the load off our feet; we sit down on the chairs along the wall. In the meantime, more people arrive clutching bunches of documents and then spread out toward the doors of the other offices.

The lobby is getting pretty full by the time our escort reappears. He gestures to Lad, giving him the go-ahead into the office telling us to be patient.

"The Regal I.D. is made here. And you will be informed of further things to do when your turn comes."

In a few minutes Lad comes waltzing out to the lobby with a bunch of official forms in one hand and a strange-looking, greenish card with a thick plastic coating.

"That's what I look like," he flashes it to each one of us, finally poking a finger at me. I'm next.

A young lady is waiting for me. She slips a form before me, asking me to sign on the dotted line. Next she directs me to a green cross on the floor.

"Look into the camera! Fine. I believe we're all done." Her hands jump from one knob to another with lightning speed. She pulls the photographic paper out of the instrument and folds it in one move. Then, without missing a beat, she feeds fresh roll of film in, pulls a switch initiating a murmuring sound. She looks up at me. It's only now that I discover how beautiful she is.

"When you people are done here go to the photographic studio across the railroad tracks where you'll have your pictures taken. You don't have to take anything else with you except the Regal ID card. Yours is already finished." She glances at her machine with a professional smile flickering across her face.

She shoves the greenish plastic in my hand. A melancholy face looks back at me from it. And yet I tried to smile, I say to myself.

"Anything wrong?" she asks.

"No, no. Everything's fine," I pocket the card.

"Please, wait for your friends, keep together as a group. When you come back with the document you get in the photo studio and the forms you have to fill out report to office number three. There you will be instructed as to the next step in this process. Send in someone else from your group!"the young lady commands while preparing the camera for a renewed use. As an afterthought she looks at me with her deep blue eyes: "Leave your luggage in storage while going about this business. Office number eight at the end of the corridor."

I hobble out of the place with my head hanging low. There's pain in my hip. I take a look at the forms in my hand, but before I can set my mind on the task of scrutinizing them, Whiskers sidles up to me.

"Screw it, there's trouble," he's jerking his arms in my face in a tizzy.

"Wait a sec," I calm him and send Mathman in before turning back to Whiskers. "Now let's hear what's happening."

"Lad has skipped out, screw it. He said he'd had enough, screw it, he's going home."

"What do you mean?"

"He said, screw it, he was heading for the border."

"And you let him? Why didn't you try to talk some sense into him?"

"I did my best, screw it, but there was no one around to help me. Don't you think we should report it to someone?"

"And what are we going to say?"

"How should I know? You're more into these things, screw it."

I stand with my head in my hands. Report what and to whom?

"Leave him to his fate," I mutter defeated. "There's nothing we can do for him. If we alert the guards, they may intercept him and arrest him. But on what charges? He has a valid ID, a Regal card."

"Screw it, you're right," Whiskers calms down. "I didn't think of that, screw it."

The cops lounging at the gate give us directions to the photo studio; it's only another short hike.

A teenage boy receives us. He takes our ID cards and leads us one by one to into the bright flood light reflected by the whitewashed back wall of the studio. My turn comes after Mathman. I'm directed to a chair in the middle of a slightly raised podium. I am blinded by the flood lights facing me. I'm left alone in a fog, a milky white fog.

* * * *

I'm trudging beside my bicycle. Plastic shopping bags are hanging from the handlebar. My wife did the shopping at the produce market, and now I deliver the goods. I'm pushing the vehicle by the sidewalk in a lousy mood. It was less than a week ago that the Securitat, the state security, let me out of their cellar. They threatened me with death. I've had little sleep ever since then. Serenity has left me for distant parts. My mind has been invaded by disquieting and strange thoughts. I'd like to calm my disturbed soul, but what can I say? Despair has become my constant companion. Among the passersby I notice a teacher of mine from high school. I greet him in a low voice.

"You here?" he looks at me as if seeing a ghost. "You look pale."

"I have little reason to rejoice," I remark quietly.

"I've heard what had happened to you. I'm very sorry for you, very sorry. What atrocious charges! Simply atrocious!" he tilts his head from side to side. "But they're after me too, peaking and whispering. Well, I'll have to say goodbye here. May Heaven be with you," he says departing from me as if I had suffered from an infectious disease.

Despair overwhelms me again.

Where can I gather the strength to crawl out of this dark pit I've fallen into? *'We cannot avoid birds flying over our heads, but we can prevent them from nesting in our hair.'*

"Dear God, lead me out of this endless forest of fears!" I catch myself whispering.

* * * *

"No need to whisper," the photographer informs me while futzing with the camera three meters away. "But never mind, just stay as you are. That's it, thank you, you can get up now."

We march back to the front part of the store.

"The mugshots I took are for your new passports. The receipt I give you is to be filed with your immigration application in the registration office," explains the photographer as he hands us each a stamped slip of paper.

"I don't get it. Why do I need a new passport if the one I have is good for another three years?" Mathman is fuming, but not until we are out in the street, headed for the Regal.

"One size fits all here. Screw it," Whiskers is ready with the explanation. "Why would you be an exception, screw it? Can't hurt to have an extra passport photo, screw it."

As we find out on our return, the next office, no. 3, has its own separate waiting room. Four tables, each with four chairs. We settle down to one of them. We have to fill out our immigration applications.

From somewhere a fortyish bespectacled blond lady appears every now and then. She checks on our progress, answers questions, and explains why accuracy is especially important in certain cases.

I'm the first one to finish. I scan the forms in front of me. I get so immersed in the task that I am not aware of the blond lady standing behind me.

"I see you're all done. Come into the office," she addresses me.

As soon as I enter, she points to a chair. I hand over the forms and the stamped slip of paper concerning the passport photo.

I watch her face, the slight changes of expression as she reads.

Suddenly she tilts her head back to look at me.

"Were they really serious when they threatened you?"

"Yes, very much so."

The memory of it is a crumpled sheet of paper.

A little while later she asks again.

"Why Australia? Why do you want to go there?"

"Because it's the farthest."

"Farthest from what?"

"From myself."

"What? From yourself?"

"From my prior life. I want twenty-four-hour flying time between me and my old life. So that it would not even cross my mind to return."

"What if they don't accept you?"

"I don't know. Why wouldn't they?"

"You can't take it for granted."

"What would they have against me?"

"A thousand and one reasons. Here, would-be immigrants can only apply and not put in orders."

"I didn't count on that."

"What did you expect?"

"I figured my persecution was a good enough reason for being accepted."

"But that's not how the real world works."

"But how does it work?"

"It's moved by invisible forces. You cannot count on logic. Rationality has no chance confronting real life. It's one thing what we believe and hope for, but what actually happens is something else."

"What's the use of setting criteria?"

"Forget criteria! They are for labeling people, that's all. But that doesn't mean we have to judge them by the label. Evaluation is a subjective decision, not a law. Canons were not invented for mortal human beings. Consequently, it can happen that you may fit the criteria in every respect, and yet you'll not be judged accordingly."

"Isn't there any way around that?"

"Yes, I believe so. Spreading your bets is the best way around it. I suggest you register with one more country. For example, Canada. If Australia doesn't come across, you don't have to languish at the Regal for another few long months waiting for another interview."

"It's all right with me," I sigh, giving in, "but this turn of events is something I did not foresee."

She produces a new set of forms from the desk drawer.

"Fill these out," she hands me the papers. "And send in one of your pals."

I take my seat again at the waiting room table. The hall is almost full by now.

I feel let-down and roll the pen between my thumb and forefinger, lost in reverie. Can't think of anything to substantiate my request.

Several precious minutes go by, but then I force myself to get down to business. The rubrics of the form quickly fill up as if by magic. Soon I have another immigration application in my hands.

"We're finished here," Mathman stops by my side. "I'm going to the residential departure unit. I'm not ready to leave yet. The job in communication technology didn't pan out. I'm staying."

"Screw it, try to get a bed in the same room with us," Whiskers somehow lets a smile creep under his mustache.

"What room are you in?"

"We don't know yet, screw it, but in a few minutes we will." Then he turns to me, "You want us to come back for you?"

"Yes," I agree to the sudden offer of friendship. "Just one of you will do…"

"I will," Mathman pats my shoulder. "I'm not hungry. Once we're settled, I'll send Whiskers to the mess hall and I'll walk back for you."

"The blond lady receives me with the formality of a true bureaucrat. She takes the papers and immediately immerses herself in them.

I pass the time looking at the view. The window looks out on a hillside. Gray clouds are settled over the landscape. They filter out the sunshine, letting through just enough to dispel the observer's melancholy.

It must be around noon. The pain is not shooting though my hip, only numbing it.

* * * *

By afternoon we're all set. True to his promise Mathman reserved the bunk over his for me.

"I don't know if you like nose-bleed heights for your sleeping accommodations, but this was the last one available," he keeps looking at me as if waiting for an answer.

66

I climb slowly and gingerly to the upper berth. I lie down flat. It has acceptable springs and the mattress is not too lumpy.

"There's more light up here," I pronounce my judgment, placing my brown case beside me.

I take a survey of the dormitory. Eight steel-framed double bunks are lined up against two walls. There is some space between them though to reach the tin locker cabinets separating them.

More of the same kind of lockers placed along the back walls and long refectory-style tables with chairs in the middle complete the furniture of the dormitory room.

I take a count of the capacity.

Thirty-two.

But there's plenty of room for more, the ceiling must be at least four meters high, I estimate.

Opposite the double-door entrance three large windows pour light inside.

In the back there's a beat-up old TV set showing silent snow while a small radio is blasting away on top of a cabinet. It's early afternoon and I see only three or four new faces in the dorm. Before I can make my way to them to introduce myself Whiskers pops out from behind a bunk asking me if I have taken a locker yet; there are still a few empty.

No, I say, I want to buy a padlock first.

"Let's go and do it now, screw it."

Mathman joins us too.

"I can hardly wait to get outside. I'm starved."

This is the third time today that we flash the Regal card to the guards camped out by the gate.

After all the trials and tribulations, it feels good to belong somewhere, even if it's the Regal. With the uncertainty of the recent past still fresh in my memory it fills me with boundless joy to savor this moment, however strange that may sound.

Something is under way.

It's possible to make plans for the future.

There is a future.

It's impossible to plan without enthusiasm, I nurse the thought, but in these happy moments I have no idea what's ahead of me, of us. My thoughts carry me back home. I think about my abandoned family, their despair, and uncertainty.

What I'm doing is for their sake as well as mine. This thought allows me to find momentary peace of mind.

* * * *

Step by step we explore the streets of this small suburban town of Vienna, the last stop on the suburban railroad, which is something between a train and a streetcar. The center seems to grow out of the railroad station. Well-maintained buildings and tasteful store window displays greet us with a friendly welcome. We can't help stopping and admiring the merchandise.

What we're looking for though is a cozy little restaurant. We check out one place after another, but none of them meet with our approval.

We're already passing the third block when Whiskers spots a pleasant-looking pub-like restaurant with a sidewalk café under parasols.

We enter in high spirits.

About half the tables are occupied, one of them has two girls sitting there.

To my surprise I notice they're speaking our native tongue. Mathman is quicker on the take. He's at their table at once.

"Hello ladies," he sits down waving to us to follow.

The first question that concerns the girls is whether we too are from the Regal. They're staying in the female pavilion.

The black-haired one with bright eyes focuses her attention on Mathman.

"I'm Teenie," she holds out a hand.

"And Blondie here," says the other girl looking at Whiskers and me.

We introduce ourselves and tell the big story of our getting out of the holding pen. They've been out for two months and working. Teeny cleans a diner where she spends all day. Blondie lost her job at a coffee packaging company just last week but has found a new one at a bakery. She's to start tomorrow.

We ask for beer. Everything on the menu looks appetizing. All three of us order something. My choice is steak Tartar with fried bread.

By the time we leave the place Teenie and Mathman are holding hands and so are Blondie and Whiskers, walking side by side as if tied together by old friendship.

In the course of our conversation the girls prove themselves a goldmine of information.

The first thing we learn is that officially we are not allowed to take jobs. If we still want to work, we have to stand out in the plaza in front of the Regal as early as possible, preferably at dawn. Later the line gets much too long. The locals pick workers from the line for day jobs according to face, appearance and sympathy. This time of the year most of them need help with grape harvesting. They expect the hireling to do a day's job. If they find someone's performance unsatisfactory, they choose someone else the next day. At noon they serve the standard fare: a fried sausage with bread and potatoes plus the obligatory bottle of beer. Sometimes they keep you working late into the evening, but then they pay extra.

It's advisable to buy a ticket for the local trains, because they are often inspected. If you're caught without a ticket, you're to pay a heavy fine, and you'll be reported to the camp administration. If you're smart, you don't take a chance. The female pavilions are open to visitors only till nine in the evening. After that time males are forcibly ejected and reported to camp security. That can mean another black mark against your name when it comes to immigration interviews.

Within the Regal several cartels operate. They control all kinds of trade taking place in the camp, whether it concerns trafficking in food, booze or narcotics. In the name of order and tranquility, the Regal administration turns a blind eye on this informal business activity. The rumor is they get their share in the profit.

Letters and packages can be picked up in a small post office by the recipients whose names are posted on a bulletin board at the corner of the main building. Others have no reason to loiter in the post office.

The food is acceptable. Warm meals are ladled out three times a day in the central mess hall. Those who don't fancy the cuisine should go to work and buy in town whatever tickles their palate.

It is also whispered that the intelligence agencies of various Eastern European countries send their operatives to the camp to gather information on their ex-compatriots.

Immigration to Canada is the fastest. Those who register with Australia and the US have to wait months and months before they can get their visa to enter.

Above all, remember this is a motley crowd. Boys, be on your guard, don't ever pick a fight with anyone, don't offend anyone, don't even argue with anyone, don't make enemies! Instead, be prepared to swallow your loss, if you have to, because you can never tell who is whose friend or business partner. These people never forgive. There was an incident when they chased after a poor fellow who neglected to pay for his bottle of beer and ran over him in the park in a deadly crash. Avoid ruckus at any cost. For men in search of women – here Teenie looks at Mathman – don't go to the Regal, because…

"Because you never know who is whose chick," Blondie kisses Whiskers on the lips and runs off ahead.

Sadness comes over me. I feel so much alone. I don't fit into this group of merrymakers. They wasted no time forming two couples. Two allied as a couple can weather any difficulty with more endurance and success than one person alone. But none of them makes me feel unwanted. Blondie smiles at me several times almost as if asking forgiveness for not choosing me. And I smile back at her. She picked Whiskers after learning that I'm married with two children. Whiskers is single, less problematic.

By late afternoon sunshine breaks through the clouds. I take a deep breath, savoring the scent of fall.

Lonely roadside trees are staring into the distance.

There's no one to hold my hand, no one whose shoulders I can hug.

* * * *

We open the door to Room No. 6, main building, the Regal, totally unsuspecting the scene that is waiting for us there. Whiskers gets hit with a pillow before we can figure out what's going on. And it's more than a pillow fight, it's a no-holds-barred brawl among the residents of the room. As we find out later it all started with a trivial dispute. When things simmer down, we finalize the act of moving in.

I place tooth paste, soap in the locker cabinet and secure it with the padlock I purchased earlier the day. I wrap the roll from the restaurant in a paper bag, hoping it will not dry out by next day.

The punching and kicking have stopped but the noise is totally out of control. Both the TV set and the radio are blaring at full volume, one in one end of the dorm and the other in the other end. With the exception of a few younger men sitting at a table everyone is speaking loudly, or rather hollering as if trying to outshout everyone else.

Two young men come up to my bed. The short balding introduces himself as Baldy and his tall and lean friend with a full head of dark hair as Wiseman. "For my parental concern", he explains. They're thirtyish, and want to immigrate to America.

In a few words I sketch out my personal history in exchange for theirs. In addition, they have further advice on life at the Regal.

71

I'm tired and worn out. The weather forecast on the radio talks about a storm forming west of us. It may get here by tomorrow. Gale-force winds, downpours at the worst time; I was hoping to try my luck on Work Plaza in front of the Regal. Maybe it'll veer off to the south, I tell myself, still hoping.

Mathman makes a curtain around his bunk. His desultory words seem to convey his disgust with the ear-piercing noise. I climb up to my place in the upper bunk. A jolt of pain again in my hip. Tomorrow I'll have to check out the infirmary and have my wound attended to. I pull the blanket over my head. It does little about the noise but at least it keeps the mercilessly bright ceiling light from burning up my eyes. I try to still the outside world inside myself.

The loneliness makes me overly sensitive and vulnerable; it's easy for me to retreat into myself.

* * * *

Squatting in the dark cornfield. Bolts of lightning follow one another in quick succession, cutting open the flesh of the landscape. Rain is coming down like a waterfall. Must get moving, I keep telling myself. Gathering all my strength, I rise and look for the lights, but my view is obstructed by cornstalks. I cautiously make my way among them in what I believe to be forward direction, but the fully-grown leaves do not only rustle but snap at my face with a crack. The farther I go the louder the cracks get, lacerating my mind and kicking my heart out of its seat.

Better stop, listen and weigh the situation.

It seems I am not alone among the cornstalks.

Between two thunders I hear a crack nearby without me moving. It's followed by more, from all around. The noise takes a dark shape rising above me and throws itself on me. Its weight knocks me to the ground. It's a growling big hound, wrestling me with its teeth.

I hear approaching voices, a shout.

The world around is embroiled in a desperate struggle.

72

"Don't let go of him! Hold him!"

The dog is lying on my chest, breathing into my face. Then there's face over us, looking down, sneering.

"Wretched jerk!"

Indeed, I pitifully scream for mercy.

Until the dog opens its jaws around my throat.

Then I'm hit in the ribs. And on my head. I lose consciousness. It's in a dingy, dirty room that I come to. My feet and hands are tied up.

"Where did you think you were running off to, you miserable creature, you?"

I can't see the man talking to me, my eyes are glued shut. My head hurts. Blows land on my shoulder and into my stomach. I howl for help.

"Wake up, wake up, what's with you? What are you yelling about? You gone crazy?"

Mathman is standing by my bed.

Light floods my eyes.

"They've got me, they'll kill me," I whisper.

"Who got you?"

"At the border. They've captured me, they'll kill me."

"Calm down," Mathman places a hand on my arm. "You're safe. At the Regal. Can you hear me?"

I open my eyes again. I look around me shamefaced. Now there are three of them standing by my bed.

"Screw it, stop spooking us. You're giving us the willies, screw it. Fancy that, screw it."

* * * *

The morning finds me with a heavy head. An unpleasant sensation comes over me. I try to recall the events of last night. Slowly the fog lifts. Pictures flicker through my mind.

"You sure gave us a proper fright last night," Mathman mutters on seeing me. "Hollering and screaming for help, till you woke up the whole place."

73

"Sorry about that," I bow my head in agreement. "I had a bad dream."

Sheaves of morning light pass dancing in front of my eyes.

The wash basin is a filthy long trough, water pours, drips, gurgles into it from a row of faucets. The stench surrounds me like a thick cloud. I squeeze extra paste on my toothbrush and start brushing vigorously.

Wearing rubber boots and gloves two young men enter with buckets and mops in their hands. They throw themselves at the washrooms. The stench is masked by the nose-twisting, eye-burning smell of chlorine. I quickly finish up.

It's seven thirty, and it's raining. The center of the storm seems to have veered off from us. On the window panes fat raindrops go racing down.

Here I am with a broken nose and wounded hip, hanging out at the Regal without my family, alone, mired in the woes of an aspiring immigrant. Last night I frightened my fellow residents with my nightmares.

I should write home, but I feel incapable of it. Let me try getting work first.

Mathman says he's got plenty of money, he doesn't have to undertake menial labor. Whiskers is sleepy. He blames me for it. Baldy, however, asks me if I feel like joining him at the day-jobbers' plaza. The two of us walk out the Regal gate and get in line about twenty meters away.

It's still drizzling, but who cares. Cars stop by at irregular intervals. Mostly women do the picking. In less than ten minutes Baldy and another fellow are seated in a sedan pulling a trailer. He beckons to me, but the lady doing the hiring waves me off.

Left behind.

The line is rapidly getting shorter. No one seems to want me though. I reach into my pocket. I count the money left after yesterday's lunch and several minor purchases. It's not much. I have no choice, I must get a job.

At nine o'clock there are still eleven of us standing on the sidewalk. We silently eye one another. I wonder what the others think of me. Am I in bad shape? Is that why no one wants me?

What difference does it make what they think? Work is what I need. No point in meditating over the question why I don't get hired.

A car comes to a halt. At the same moment the rain gets heavier. I've got no hat, no umbrella. The man in the car beckons to me.

"Stacking firewood, okay with you?"

"Yes," I don't even think about the answer.

I take the backseat. A young woman sits behind the wheel. I say good morning, but she doesn't respond. We drive only five blocks before we stop in front of a tidy two-storey home. We get out without a word. The rain turns to a slow drizzle again.

The man hurries ahead to open the gate for the car and then to a storage shed in the back. It's packed with firewood, the logs arranged in neat order.

"This is what you have to carry from here," and we walk across the backyard to the boiler room, "to here." He points to a willow basket and the space where I'm supposed to stack the logs. I can get to Work.

The rain has stopped in the meantime.

It takes two rounds for me to arrive at the number of logs to put in the basket in such a way as not to kill myself and still get the job done in good time. By the third round I achieve the perfect balance. From then on I can work mechanically, without giving it another thought. The prospect of money in my pocket lifts my spirit. I plan on buying stationary tonight and sending my first letter home.

I start writing it in my mind, but I can't get beyond the first line. What can I say to them? Surely not the truth. I can't share with them the suffering I had to go through in the past few days.

At noon the man comes out and takes a look at the stacks. From his sober nod I infer he's satisfied with my progress. In a few minutes he appears again bringing a plate and a bottle of beer. He puts them on the porch table. I wash my hands in the boiler room.

Through the kitchen door left open I can see they too sit down to lunch.

I gobble up my meal without much enthusiasm, yet it's not bad. Sausage with sautéd cabbage. The bread is fresh, its crust is crackly.

I start working again. Going back for the second load after lunch I notice my employers still sitting at the kitchen table.

They don't consider a Regalist human, they don't invite that ostracized foreign pariah to their table; the thought comes to haunt my mind. But how would I act in their place? I ask myself with a bitter smile slipping across my lips. Surely not like this, not like this, I keep reassuring myself silently.

I finish the job by two in the afternoon.

The man nods with satisfaction and gives me fifty more than what he offered in the morning. Calls out the young woman. We get in the car and drive back to the Regal.

The guards stop me at the gate. They seem to be on edge, but then I notice more of them running around. Soon there are three of us waiting to be admitted. A uniform with a sub-machinegun in hand runs across the quadrangle. We get no information on what's going on inside. Soon everyone is on edge.

After a while an officer comes to the gate and checks our passes with a nod. The two other residents make their way to the registration building, and I veer off in the direction of the main building. In front of the entrance I see a police car and an ambulance. Both have their lights blinking.

Good heavens, what's happened? My heart is throbbing in my throat. After a few more steps I see the men in white coats on top of the stairs carrying a steel-frame bed.

Coming closer I can also see a man lying on the bed with a kitchen knife in his chest.

Horrified, I don't know how to react. Finally decide to head for the entrance if no one stops me.

I'm but a few meters from the ambulance. The paramedics are endeavoring to transfer the knifed man from the bed to the gurney. Two policemen hurry to their help. The man on the bed is just lying there quietly. There is no whimper from him. His face is deadly pale.

I run up the stairs. I meet Whiskers halfway up.

"What's happened?"

"What did you expect, screw it?"

"Who got stabbed?"

"Screw it, how should I know?"

"They just carried him off, bed and all."

"Relax, pal, you'd better get used to this, screw it. And go to the registration office, screw it, find Madam Olga, she sent for you, screw it."

"Madam Olga? Who's that?"

"The lady who took our immigration applications."

I'm afraid to turn back. Instead I turn into my dorm. A few regulars are lounging on beds, the radio is blaring.

I climb up to my bed.

Waiting for the moment to pass.

* * * *

"My employment contract has been nullified," I mumble looking in my wife's eyes with sorrow.

"The same old issues?"

"Yes. Nothing related to work, my performance. Only the same old issues: antisocial statements, offensive to the basic tenets of communism; subversive activity, dissemination of enemy propaganda, radical nationalist manifestations detrimental to the unity of the country," I cite various items from the long list as they come to my mind.

"My God, what is to become of us?"

"Hard to tell right now. We move to the country. We pack up, gather the kids and move in with your aunt on the hillside."

"What if she refuses to take us in?"

77

"Then we have to think of something else. At the moment this is the only solution I can think of. You should've seen how thick my dossier was. When our secretary was pushing it toward me to sign for its receipt, I asked her: Is this all about me? All these accusations are against me? She looks at me and dropped her eyelids."

"What kind of a future is waiting for our children if we cannot properly provide for them? With their father and mother deprived of work opportunities?"

"I don't know what else to do. Not in the short term."

"And how about the director? Did he too speak against you?"

"No. He was the only one who remained silent. But even that can be hazardous. Silence can be taken for approval. Conspiracy."

"What are we going to live on?"

"One can always find work in the country. This thing may blow over in a few years and we can return to the city. But please, don't tell my mother. She gets so anxious about the smallest things."

"And where are the kids going go to school?"

"In the country. Who knows, they might even benefit from the fresh country air and the change of scenery."

"You have an answer for everything. But what about their circle of friends, the community that they belong to?"

"They'll develop new friendships and join a new community. Come to your senses, this is not the biggest problem facing us. Don't you think I'm just as upset as you, and don't you..."

My wife bursts into tears.

I can't bear the weight of my heart. I feel like running away. In a cloak of invisibility. I can't stand seeing her cry. I ask her to stop. But she won't. Keeps on crying, letting me have it.

* * * *

By the time I make it down to the steps of the building again it's completely deserted. Far off, in the lap of the hilly horizon, the shadow of a melancholy afternoon is prowling.

I cut across the empty quadrangular court heading for the registration office.

The corridor is quiet.

"I didn't notice yesterday that you failed to sign one of the application forms," Madam Olga greets me cordially, bidding me to take a seat.

She places the document in front of me and points to the dotted line with a X beside it.

I give her a report on my first day working. Talking about it now, I find it quite positive.

"When are they going to submit the applications?"

"Tomorrow or the day after. First I have to check each one for missing or contradictory data; anything out of order will cause the application to be returned for correction and we end up with more delays."

"How long does it take for them to respond?"

"It varies according to the number of applications and the number of administrators working on them at any given time. The average response time is three to four weeks. Those they want to consider they invite for an interview. That will determine the outcome."

"And do they explain the reasons for a rejection?"

"No. The decision is final, and the applicant does not have the right to appeal. Look at it this way: it's a human resources market. If you're young, with a family, educated, an expert in a special field the recipient country is interested in, you have a good chance of being accepted. But don't get your hopes up. That's why I asked you to apply to two countries. One out of two is almost a sure bet. One of them is bound to take you. It's like a lottery. If you're lucky you can be sitting on a plane in two months."

"And how about my family? When can they join me?"

"That too depends on luck. But you can submit their application only after you get to your new country."

"Each step takes time and more time!"

"Unfortunately, yes. It's a game of patience."

I look out the window.

"It's hard to be patient," I unintentionally raise my voice a bit.

"One can learn, if there's no other choice."

"That applies to me," I observe more calmly.

"Look in on me someday when you feel up to it. I read in your bio you worked as a decorator, too. Don't you think my office could use a decorator's touch?"

"Very much so," I look around with an appraising eye.

"Another thing. I almost forgot it. Tomorrow morning you'll have to report to the green pavilion for medical examination. Tell your friends, too. Actually, an announcement about it will be posted on the bulletin board," saying this she gets to her feet to show me out. "How is your hip? Still aching?" she asks from the door.

"It bothered me some while lugging firewood. I'll go to the infirmary from here," I reply and hand the door latch to an incoming client.

When I checked it out in the mirror in the morning some blood was seeping through the bandage. Otherwise it was fine, did not hurt worse than before.

* * * *

After I'm finished with the infirmary a livelier picture waits for me in the court. It's filled with residents getting back from work.

Looks like it's about to rain again.

I run into Mathman at the entrance to the main building.

"I hear you've been working," he pats my shoulder. Come, let's visit the girls. Whiskers says you were there when the ambulance picked up the bartender."

"What bartender?"

"The one who got stabbed in the chest. At the Regal several unlicensed bartenders operate," he started his lecture. "On the third floor there are two of them. While you were out, I covered the whole building, that's how I've learned. Those who operate these private liquor stores are called bartenders. They sell beer, wine, vodka, whiskey, just about everything. The perp was supposedly drunk. Rumor has it that in the past five days he's been drinking steadily because his application is refused by every possible place. It was last week that he got the word, it was all over, no way out, he'll have to rot at the Regal to the end of his days. The bartender refused to extend him credit. Eyewitnesses say they had often quarreled in the past. This afternoon the perp went back with the promise of paying off his debt, but instead he stabbed the bartender in the chest. And here we are at the girls' pavilion. Is this your first time here?"

"Why do you expect me to know everything?" I give Mathman a dirty look. "I've been working all day long; I haven't had the time to explore the Regal."

We step into a room with eight beds in it. They too are stacked up, like ours.

The first thing we see is a couple in embrace. Blondie pulls away from Whiskers's arms, looking impish. She fixes her rumpled blouse. Teenie jumps into Mathman's arms putting hers around his neck where she stays hanging in titters.

"Sit down. How about coffee?" Blondie looks at me.

"I'll have a cup too, screw it."

"In that case I'll put on another pot," Blondie slips out of the room, soon to return with a preserve jar filled with water.

Slowly the mood of the room thaws. Coffee comes to boil. We encircle the table with our chairs.

Whiskers reports someone offered him a broken-down, old jalopy for sale.

"And what would you do with it, if it's broken-down and old?"asks Mathman with tact.

"What do you expect, screw it? I'll make out with Blondie in it."

"With me, in an old jalopy?"

"Why, where else did you expect me to, in a four-star hotel?"

"Hi you guys, what's the subject of the debate?" a blondish girl slips closer to the table.

"Where did you appear from?" Mathman turns his eyes on her.

"I was taking a nap, but the loud talk woke me up."

"Guys, to those of you who have not yet had the pleasure I introduce Nina," says Teenie and takes a stagy bow.

"We've already met, screw it," mutters Whiskers.

Seems to me he resents the interruption of the conversation. Nina is quiet. She doesn't like Whiskers' behavior.

"Children, children, my situation is the most disadvantaged. Four of you at least have a partner. But where am I?" I look around the table with a deadpan face.

"Here's Nina for you, a photo model. Perfect figure, blond hair, blue eyes. She's yours, screw it," Whiskers goes on with his bluster.

"Me? Out of question," Nina is annoyed. "I'm no slut!"

"Who the hell said you were, screw it? Here's this guy," he nods toward me, "he knows how to stick it in. Don't you like to stick it in, screw it?" he shouts toward me.

"I've had enough of this," Nina gets up from the table and walks out of the dorm looking straight ahead.

"What were you trying to prove?" Blondie playfully boxes Whiskers' shoulder.

"What was I trying prove? Screw it, I'll tell you. She thinks just because she's a beauty queen," he stops here to look at each one of us at the table one by one, "she's so-so special, screw it. We happen to be sitting at the Regal where we're all equal, screw it. Everyone makes out with everyone else. How come she doesn't, screw it?"

"Have you been drinking?" Blondie acts shocked.

"Do I look like it? Haven't I been with you all afternoon, screw it?"

"Then why did you get so worked up?"

"Because, screw it, I don't like hypocrites, screw it. She waltzes in here, pops her eyes, complains of us for talking too loud and waking her up. Instead of sitting down with us like a normal person and talking to us nicely, screw it."

"Don't get so worked up. Five weeks ago, before she came to the Regal she had a miscarriage, she lost a baby from the man she loved more than anything in the world," Blondie relates, slapping Whiskers' face with her fine hand.

"That's another story, but how was I to know, screw it?"

"You know what?" Blondie slips into Whiskers' lap, "Go ahead, buy that broken-down old jalopy, and I promise here in front of witnesses that after the first test drive I'll let you stick it in."

* * * *

Today's earnings allow me to purchase stationary. I spend some time standing in front of shelves of neat envelopes and letter paper in all colors and sizes. I tend toward the apple green and pink, but it's hard to decide between the two. Although I like its shading, I finally I decide against the pink because its mawkishness. I pick the green. The cashier is a high school girl. She keeps shifting her gaze, apparently in an effort to avoid meeting mine. Does she guess I'm from the Regal and that's why she's acting so strange? I ask myself, but the transaction is consummated in short order and the next moment finds me in the street.

This evening I don't feel like eating in the mess hall, and in the morning I enjoy coffee rather than tea, the only thing served there. The food store is crowded. By their looks most customers are from the Regal, like me. I put rolls, butter, cold cuts, jam, sugar, instant coffee, milk and a mug in which to warm up the last item.

On the way home I almost get blown away by the wind.

Shivers shoot through my body.

The icy wind penetrates to my skin.

Late afternoon it stops raining but the air gets colder. The weather forecast calls for the return of warmer weather for the weekend.

* * * *

Blinding lights, blasting music, cigarette smoke, pandemonium fill the dorm when I enter. After I put my stuff away, I get out of the wet dark blue jacket. There's a group standing in one end, mostly boys in their early twenties. The subject of their debate is who should qualify for immigration on the fast track.

The scrawny one among them may not even be twenty.

The way they talk it soon becomes clear that they all have steady work. A barber works a long shift in the neighboring small town every Saturday. He gets home at midnight. His desired destination is America while his friends aim at Canada. The present subject of their debate is the number of points each has racked up in his favor. It seems immigration permits are handed out based on a point system. I soon stop trying to follow their analysis, which criteria command how many points. What can I do to improve my chances if my life is to be judged by such rigid, impersonal standards? This system practically calls for fudging the data or even outright prevarication.

It slowly emerges that the barber is generally disliked by the roommates. They're envious of him, his lucrative job and his free-spending excursions on Sundays. Sometimes he doesn't get back until Monday evening, he has that day off, too.

In addition, the barber is suspected of being a stoolpigeon for the authorities. He must be spying on the residents since he's always circulating in the building when he's around. Obviously, he's keeping a tab on everyone. Once he was caught checking on suspected drug users – which he vehemently denies. The only problem is he cannot explain why the three druggies were hauled off by the police the very next day.

We're well into this kind of chatter when Wiseman comes to the table with a funny look on his face. He takes hold of my arm and asks me to join him for a little walk.

"Don't get mixed up with this bunch," he whispers into my ear as we amble away. "They're trouble-makers. And there's someone else to stay away from, an older man. Must be past forty, but still has curly hair. The barber takes care of his coiffeur. He's out now, usually gets back after eleven, drunk as a skunk. I've never seen him sober. He, too, is suspected of spying on us."

I must look frightened in the extreme, because he's taken aback.

"But there's no need to panic. I merely wanted to bring you up to date on our room population. The best policy is to keep to yourself. In this case it's true that what you don't know cannot hurt you. The less you know the better."

Thanking his advice, I return to my bed. Mathman's spot is empty. I spread out my supper there. I eat quickly and then move up to my bunk to write home. Climbing up I feel pain shooting into my hip again. They changed the bandage in the afternoon, but it still itches. The skin feels tight. I have the pen in my hand.

"My Loved Ones, I am well. I filled out and submitted my immigration application. Today I even got work and earned a little money. I have food to eat and a place to sleep. I'll try calling you in the next few days. I'd like to hear your voices. Millions of kisses, your loving father.

Write to me as much as you can!"

I slip the folded letter in the envelope, and quickly, before I can change my mind, lick the edge and seal it.

It's hard to fall asleep while being assaulted by light and noise. I try to remove myself mentally from my surroundings, set my mind free. But every time I am about drop off something yanks me back into the bitter reality of wakefulness.

* * * *

Sunshine resting on my pillow wakes me up.

Some in the room are already up, listlessly rummaging in their lockers. Looking down, I see Mathman sleeping with his face covered with a scarf. Today I cannot sell my labor on the plaza. I have a medical exam this morning at ten o'clock. Sitting up I get hit in the chest by an invisible blow. I try swinging my left arm but it aches even more intensely before the pain dissipates.

Perspiration collects under my watchband that I neglected to take off for the night.

It's four minutes to eight.

In the clinic I count forty people waiting, and there are more pouring in through the wide-open door. By the time they call the first group there isn't enough space left to place two more feet on the floor.

From the people around me I find out they are not all new arrivals. Many are coming from the surrounding hotels. Refugees who were lucky enough not to have been put up at the Regal.

Pretty soon the crowd dwindles down to one half. We have plenty of room to walk around, and we take advantage of the opportunity to make acquaintances and learn from one another's experiences.

In one corner a young mother is hanging on to her small daughter who seems to be eager to break free. The mother is talking to a middle-aged lady until the little girl manages to pull her hand free and go sprinting down the hall. I catch her and lift her playfully up in the air.

"I have two little boys at home," I escort the child to the mother. "They are just as rambunctious, it's a nonstop running race."

All three of them are residing in a quiet hotel ten kilometers away. Their board is very satisfactory, and they are in fresh air in that mountain resort. The young woman left her husband behind in their native land when on an escorted excursion west of the Iron Curtain she stepped off the bus in an unguarded moment. The middle-aged lady is an opera singer. She came abroad to sing a role, and then decided not to go home. Then it's my turn to tell the adventurous story of my daring escape. They give me their address just in case I have a chance to visit their resort town.

The medical examination is a very hurried, routine affair. They open a medical record for me that contains all the immunizations I received and remember. I complain of the pressure I've felt in my chest since this morning. The doctor listens to my chest and shrugs; nothing wrong with me, he hears no extraneous noise. I show my hip too. That too is healing nicely. Next to the X-ray room. I have to turn twice in front of the screen and cough several times. All done, I can go and dress.

Mathman is waiting for me in front of the main building. Whiskers joins us in a minute or two, all smiles.

"I'm disgustingly healthy, screw it!" his smile turns to concern though looking at me. "What's eating you?"

"He has a chest pain," Mathman answers for me.

"Didn't they look inside with x-ray? Did they find anything, screw it?"

"No, but I have the pain, a stitch, I can hardly breath."

"Must be a cold, it'll go away soon enough," Mathman makes a dismissive gesture. "Let's go and pay a visit to Teenie."

We open the door silently in case Teenie is still asleep after the nightshift. To our surprise though we find her sitting at the table with Nina.

"I thought you guys were at a medical examination," she looks up at us with a bright expression.

"It went pretty fast," we answer in unison.

Nina gets up from the table and heads inside the dorm. I get hold of her hand, asking her to stay. There are more than enough chairs for us.

Yesterday I didn't have a chance to take a good look at her. The circumstances of our introduction were not conducive to getting acquainted. Now there's no tension in the room, instead there's sunshine pouring in the window and delineating her fine features, her perfectly smooth forehead, her slender and straight nose, arched eyebrows, her long eyelashes over blue eyes, all adding up to a personification of classical beauty. My spying glances seem to embarrass her, because she turns away almost demurely. She can hide her face from me but not her body which is equally beautiful. A blue dress with a tiny flower print barely covers her knees; her wispy waist is embraced by a brown belt. The cleavage is low enough to reveal snow white breasts, relatively large for her willowy figure, pointed and very desirable.

It would be nice to gain her favors for this interim period in the camp. Whiskers is right, I do need someone to be with. But I'll have to go easy and not break down the door trying to reach out to her.

"Our friend is not quite well." Mathman points at me.

"I got a cold. It can happen to anyone. And don't forget, I crossed the border in a horrendous downpour. I got soaked to the bones. I might even have pneumonia."

"Out of the question, it would've showed up in x-ray."

"Maybe it's too early. It only started piercing my chest this morning."

"Coffee's served," Teenie places the tray on the table and then moves into Mathman's lap. "You want to stick it in?" she whispers loudly enough for all of us to hear her.

"Come up to the dorm tonight, and I'll make arrangements," Mathman continues the stage whisper.

* * * *

An afternoon walk in the Regal park. The rust-colored leaves are flapping in the wind like the freshly opened feathers of a peacock. I am walking on a thin carpet of loam, my eyes on a white contrail left by an ascending plane. I look at its path with deep longing. When am going to move on from here?

The pain piercing my chest doesn't want to cease. Before going back to my dorm I take a detour to the corner bulletin board. Although I know it's much too early for me to expect mail from home, they don't even know my address here, and it gives me vicarious pleasure to scan the roll call of those who have letters waiting for them. My name will be up there very soon. Everything comes to those who wait.

I'm determined to get a good night's rest tonight, that's my resolution for the evening. Getting to my bunk I find Mathman's place curtained off with extra bed sheets. I peek through a chink at a corner but see no one in the love nest. In the washroom I run into Teenie. I teasingly ask her if she's lost and needs directions, but she says with an impish smile Mathman is only willing to perform cunnilingus on a freshly washed pussy.

I spend the ensuing hour lying flat on my back, trying to mesmerize the ceiling with eyes frozen in open position. I hear all kinds of inarticulate but definitely human noises coming up from below, groaning and moaning, dragged out or cut short, while the whole structure keeps moving, sometimes gently rocking, sometimes shakings like it's about to come apart under me.

A grown-up man, well past the first flush of youth, I should be able deal with any situation, and yet I feel so inane, so paralyzed now. And as lonely as a sack of potatoes that had fallen off a cart, not worth anyone's while to pick it up from the mud and take home; it just rots there. Do I envy Mathman? Of course. Nina comes to mind. What would it be like to make love to her? Provided she'd agree to such flimsy accommodation? But it's been only two weeks, and am I already willing to cheat on my poor abandoned wife? On the other hand, can a man abstain without feeling like a helpless jerk?

* * * *

Back at the Regal late afternoon, next day, all worn out, after picking grapes in one of the nearby vineyards. They hired three of us off the labor plaza. The wound on the hip no longer gives trouble, but the pressure in my chest persists, making me more and more nervous. The next day and the next, the same thing. It bothers me at work to such an extent that I begin to really worry about it. Finally, I decide to go back to the doctor with it.

The place is empty. Only two people ahead of me.

I take a seat carefully, slowly, which helps me avoid the sharp pain. Apart from this discomfort I should be happy with my achievements: three days' wages earned plus two meals every day. I save on food, and put aside some cash. I'll have to send a package home as soon as I can.

The same doctor looks me over. He listens to my chest with his stethoscope, taking his time. Finally, he declares there's nothing wrong with me.

"Then why the sharp pain in my chest?" I ask, working up enough courage for the timid question.

"I don't think that's where the problem lies."

"But where?" I ask suspiciously.

"In your head," he says evenly and pauses. "It's all nerves. It's just the body's natural response to unnatural stress."

What can I say?

"Do you work?" he asks after a short silence.

"Picking grapes the last three days."

"Does it bother you while working?"

"Yes. Sometimes I can hardly move."

He produces a script pad and scribbles something on it. He rips it off and hands it to me.

"Have this filled at the pharmacy. Take it three times a day. I hope it helps."

In the court I run into Whiskers.

"I bought the vehicle, screw it. Come, let me show it to you," he puts an arm around my shoulders. "I haven't seen you in the past few days. Getting a few jobs lined up, screw it?"

"Yes," I have to free myself of his embrace, otherwise I cannot breathe.

"Still bothers you, doesn't it, screw it," he reads my movements.

"Coming from the pharmacy with a medication. The doctor prescribed a tranquilizer."

"A tranquilizer, screw it?"

"He says the trouble is not with my chest but my mind."

The dead leaves rustle under our feet as we enter the park. Among the trees my eyes light upon a big white sedan.

"A little rusty," I circle it appreciatively.

"Yes, screw it, but we had a walloping good time in it, Blondie and me. If you can use it, I'll lend it to you. Get your hands on Nina, screw it, and drag her in here," Whiskers bangs the side of the car before opening the door and showing the interior which is spacious enough for comfortable love-making.

* * * *

Yes, I'd like to have someone press against me, someone with whom I could share my body and soul.

These are the thoughts that occupy my mind, standing on the labor plaza. Now close to an hour. Waiting for someone to pick me up.

Suddenly, in a distance I glimpse Baldy waving at me. Maybe he's got something.

"Come, let's get moving! I've found work for you."

"Where?"

"In the coffee-packing plant. Three of the regular employees didn't show up this morning, and the boss asked me to bring at least one worker from the Regal."

"What's the work?"

"Packaging. Stop asking questions and start moving. I'll tell you all about it on the way."

We only have three stops to go by tram and the inspectors enter the car practically on our heels. We were tempted to get a free ride, but in the last moment we thought better of it. The fine would have been more than a day's wages. It wasn't worth the risk.

From the tram stop we have to walk three more blocks to a long one-story building with two canvas-covered tractor trailers in front of the loading dock. Electric forklifts shove cloth sacks on palettes into an opening in the wall.

In minutes we are in an office with three desks overlooking a the packaging floor through a glass wall.

The door opens, a short man in a white work coat and a woman with heavy makeup enter. We say hello but only the woman answers, her companion looks away with an expression of disgust or boredom. Or both.

"My roommate," Baldy introduces me, then adds hurriedly "reliable and hard-working fellow."

The woman pulls a sour smile.

"Did you tell him about the job?" she asks, and without waiting for an answer she launches into a long, rapidly delivered monologue. "We need you in the loading area. In a minute we'll be walking over to the stockroom, but first I want to warn you we immediately dismiss those who do not explicitly follow our instructions. Watch out for the forklifts, keep out their way. We had two accidents in the past few weeks due to the carelessness of our employees. There are managers in each section of this plant. You must obey their instructions explicitly. Every ninety minutes you can take a ten-minute coffee break. The coffee is free. Anyone caught stretching the break time is immediately sent packing. Lunch breaks are only by special permission from the manager. We have three hours to unload the trucks, so that's our first priority. If we take longer than specified in the contract the clock starts running and we must pay the delivery company a fee for overtime. We cannot afford that extra cost. Am I clear to you?" the woman gives me a cold, hard look.

"Understand," I stutter overwhelmed by the importance of the task ahead.

"Any questions?"

"I'm all set," I hurry to sound more positive.

"Let's get the show on the road," she turns to a wall cabinet for a blue work coat and slams it in hand.

I put it on. It seems short.

"Short is better, its hem doesn't get caught during bagging," she rattles off the words on our way to the stockroom.

I look around overawed. Every direction I can look I see sacks stuffed to bursting with raw coffee beans, mountains of them leaning against one another. I couldn't even imagine such concentration of coffee beans piled up in one place. Loaded forklifts glide past us at a great clip, it's a busy place. Baldy steps away for a few seconds and returns wearing his own blue coat. Our guide who turns out to bear the name Julia, hands us over to Saul, the manager of the stockroom, and disappears without further ado.

Saul gives us a cursory look.

"You know what to do."

He looks at Baldy, walking toward the loading dock where four trucks are parked with the canvas cover folded over. We direct our steps to the closest one. Only a quarter of the load remains to be unloaded. Baldy reveals the trick of getting hold of a sack and carrying it to the palette with the least expenditure of energy.

We work at a good pace, driving ourselves hard. I soon break into sweat. Although I started the day with medication, I feel renewed piercing in my chest. But by the time we toss the last sack on the palette I am so overheated that I hardly feel a thing except for a pleasant numbness all over my body.

"Coffee break!" Baldy shouts as if giving an order and turns toward the stockroom.

In the small break room there are two coffee makers. With experienced movements he fills the basket, screws it in place, and turns a lever on the side that triggers the brewing process. Two cups slowly fill up with frothing dark coffee and the small room with delicious coffee aroma.

"Milk?"

"Please." I nod.

He's already letting the cream ooze out of the box and into the cup. The finished concoction is not only fragrant but tasty, too. Rather robust. In minutes we're done with it and running back to the loading dock.

By five in the afternoon we unload three trailer trucks, a total of six of us working together. Now every part of me is numb, but I have no other complaints.

This period of time includes three coffee breaks but no lunch break, neither of us has a sandwich with us. I become aware of the aching emptiness of my stomach when we stop working.

Saul quickly shows up when we get ready to leave and stands in the door, blocking the way out.

"You fellows will have to stay yet," he raises his voice to a clarion call. 'You'll have to repack two hundred sacks."

"But we had no lunch, and we cannot go without dinner, too," even Baldy is surprised.

"That's your problem. If you don't stay on the job, don't bother to come back tomorrow morning. Understand?"

Baldy looks at me with a raised eyebrow.

"We'll stay," I give in, helplessly dropping my eyes to the floor.

"Okay, then follow me," Saul gets going with determined strides to the inner section of the stockroom.

"We'll put lots of sugar and milk in the coffee, that'll give us energy to continue," I whisper to Baldy.

We come to a mountain of sacks.

"You see these sacks? You'll have to open each one and repack its contents into a new sack from this roll," he points to a continuous roll of sacks, just like the plastic ones in a food store. He leaves us to our work.

Baldy sets up the job with expertise by lining up fifteen sacks in a row. We cut the edge at the top where the sack is stitched shut and slip a new sack over the newly made opening. By flipping the sack upside down, we completely transfer the beans into the new sack. There's a handy sewing machine for sealing the new bag which we place on a palette, ready for storage. We work as fast as we can, but in the first hour we repack only thirty sacks.

"Disgusting!" Baldy fumes lethargically, "We've hardly made a dent. At this rate we'll not get done by nine. Coffee break!"

Back in the break room he cooks the coffee for larger mugs. I put five spoons of sugar in mine and fill it to the brim with cream. In minutes we're back on the job.

By the time we finish we find ourselves alone in the enormous warehouse. Never noticed it when the race of the forklifts had stopped. On the way to the locker room I see them all lined up against the wall, plugged into a battery of large industrial electrical outlets.

"It makes me mad," Baldy growls darkly on the tram going home. "They pay us fifty shillings an hour for the repacking job, and they make at least a thousand on each sack."

"How do you figure that?"

"How, you dumb idiot?" he grunts at me, "Didn't you see we poured beans from sacks marked Brazil into ones marked Columbia? Columbian coffee fetches at least twenty percent more on the market. Can you imagine how much they made on this repacking job? And we see little of the profit."

"But at least we had a chance to work," I muse softly. "I need every penny I can make."

"Let's hope we don't get charged with conspiracy to commit fraud. And then we'll see what this great freedom is all about. The relentless growth of a free economy! What a fucked-up world!"

The tram stops. My legs can barely hold me getting off, I am so famished. Baldy runs ahead. I can't keep up.

"The food store still open?" I yell after him.

"Where do you think I'm running?" he redoubles his pace.

The noise level of the various social interactions in the dorm exceeds the usual. Curly, the man Wiseman warned me against, stands swaying by his bed.

"I'll exterminate all those shitheads!" he hollers in the direction of the younger generation. "

"You think you can just walk in any place you please while I rot here, is that it? You think I'm a limp old prick? Well, I'll have you know I have the talent, the blood in my weenie, to rise far above you, you no-good bastards!"

He takes a break from his tirade, holding on to the steel frame of the bunk with his eyes closed, looking like a boat moored to a dock in rough seas. Baldy and I go to the table with our cold cuts and bread, stuffing ourselves even before we sit down. Soon Wiseman is with us too.

"Hello, boys. Where are you coming from?"

"The coffee roasting plant," I mumble with a full mouth.

"Worked steady without a bite all day. Hungry?"

"I understand they pay well."

"Sure, sure. We're bursting with cash." Baldy snaps at the question.

"How long has this circus been on?"

"Curly got here maybe a half an hour ago. Drunk out of his mind."

"I can see that," I nod, stuffing a slice of salami in my mouth.

"Goddamit! We forgot the beer," Baldy slaps the table, turning to me. "Go to the bartender for two bottles of beer, but make sure you get the better brand, the one with gold collar around the neck!"

I'm hardly up from the table when Curly suddenly turns to me, almost tripping over his owns feet.

"And you, who the hell you think you are? You never bothered to introduce yourself. In this damned shithouse everyone's supposed to introduce himself. Where're you from, screw it?"

Baldy and Wiseman come to my rescue. They peel Curly off of me.

The second-floor bartender is out of the gold-collar bottles, I have to drag myself up to the third floor. The first corridor is dark and empty. It turns at a ninety-degree angle, and the place is the second door to the right. I knock. No answer. I wait a little. Open the door. It's the wrong place, very wrong, it's immediately clear to me. Three skin heads in all black look at me and not with a welcoming smile.

"What's wrong junior? Lost?" asks the one nearest the door.

"Yes, beg your pardon," I mumble humbly and turn to leave.

Four more skinheads jump off the beds. One of them has a rubber truncheon in his hand.

"So you've been spying on us, haven't you?" they all speak at once, as if in a well-rehearsed chorus.

Using energy reserves I didn't know, I had I run out the place. Back to the second floor. For the second-choice beer.

"Where have you been all this time?" Baldy stares at me stretching his legs out under the table, completely relaxed.

"I was looking for the gold-collared bottles, but they didn't have them on the third floor either," I place four bottles on the table.

'That's strange. They always have it on the third floor. Maybe you looked in the wrong room."

"Yes, they usually have, but now they'd run out. They'll have it again tomorrow," I try to close the subject, letting the beer gurgle down my throat.

Curly is quiet again. With eyes shut, hanging on to the steel frame of the bunk bed. Moving back and forth like a boat in harbor rocked by gentle waves.

* * * *

I am awakened by someone jerking my arm.

"Get ready, got to get going."

"Where?"

"Come on, man, get up already!" Baldy cursing softly.

In seconds I'm rushing to dress and even pack a sandwich. My head is heavy, I'm half asleep running to the tram stop.

It's still dark outside, dawn is lingering in distant regions. A cool wind slips under my shirt.

There's no sign of life in front of the coffee roasting plant. The loading gates are each a silent yawn. Baldy is not discouraged by the sight. We scamper up to the lockers.

Saul stands in the dignified pose of a field marshal with his generals before a battle. We're last to arrive.

"No new merchandise is on its way for today. What we have is the work we started yesterday, the repacking," he leads the charge into the inner regions of the stockroom.

There are eight of us now following him.

Nine hundred sacks of coffee are waiting for us, we have to repack them, that is, reassign their country of origin. The problem is we used up the sacks with Columbian insignia; two of us are sent for paint and the stencil while Baldy and I are told to look for the stitching machine. We look in every nook and cranny but can't find it. It's nowhere to be seen. We climb over several mounds of coffee sacks, but no stitching machine. Behind one of these mountains we come upon the remains of an old office. The drawers of a collapsed desk lie on the floor helter-skelter. Yellowing pages of inventories hide among the unglued wooden drawers. The frame of an ancient calculator stares at us like a skeleton. We start rummaging among the various archeological objects. The more time we pass here the stronger in me the feeling becomes that we're in the hulk of ship, sunken long ago, where time is crumbling and giving off a miasma that tickles our noses.

"This must've been their very first desk when they opened for the coffee distribution business," Baldy bangs on a board, maybe a desktop, as if testing the resilience of the wood with his fist.

"Who knows?" I try to be sociable but lack the energy. My voice is hoarse and without any sign of interest.

"Look what has become of it," he props up the board against a stack of coffee bags and goes up and down in front of it like Moses with the tablet.

We still can't find the sack stitching machine anywhere. Finally, we have to join the others without it. They're already hard at work, transferring coffee beans from one sack into another. One of them asks us where we've been hanging out. We inform him of the object of our search. They point to the corner; it's been there all the time.

We don't pick up the insane pace of yesterday. Now we're only two in a large team of workers, no point proving anything. Someone has radio blaring from the top of a stack. Our bodies and thoughts move to a slower, more humane rhythm. We're feeling good. The work keeps us alive instead of torturing us.

Around four in the afternoon Saul shows up. He scans us with his rigid gaze.

"I thought you had long finished," his arms akimbo like the slave drivers in the historical movies. His voice is sharp. "We have two truckloads of merchandise. Who wants to work overtime? And make some extra cash?"

We all bend down and scrutinize our shoes.

"If you expect me to woo you, you are gravely mistaken!"

Slowly my hand rises as if by itself. Baldy slaps it down, but it's too late. Saul has seen it.

"Good, you and who else?"

There are two more volunteers. Baldy too swings his arm high; Saul is triumphant. He looks out over us with the superiority of a boss, basking in the respect due to his office.

"You can start now," he first waves to the wretched volunteers and then toward the rest: "And you can go home. I'll subtract one hour from your wages."

Baldy looks disgusted, and there's little doubt as to the source of his irritation.

"Why the hell did you have to sign up for overtime?"

"I need the money. I must send a package to my family."

At ten at night we walk home silently side by side. I know what bothers him most: the food store is closed by now. The remains of yesterday's feast will barely fill the fare tonight; tomorrow we'll have to starve. It's only while undressing for bed I realize how numbed my body is. Every move I make is accompanied by pain. On the other hand, my chest is pain-free and has been all day even without the medication.

The glaring light of the ceiling fixture and the blaring noise fail to bother me. Mathman is asleep already, sawing away softly.

My family comes to my mind, especially the two growing children. I am missing out on an important part of their lives. But every day brings our reunion a day closer. And I've been working and earning money. Making good use of this down time in my life.

* * * *

In the morning, on the way to work, the dream of the past night comes back to me. Replaying the scene in my mind I relive it again.

I was pacing a room filled with flowers. I was waiting for Nina. She had promised to spend the whole afternoon with me. The room was not a part of a house but existed independently as a mountain peak in a sunny field that was actually a cloud cover level with the peak. I looked out the window in search of Nina.

There was no one outside.

Turning back to the room I found myself faced by her. "How did you get here?" I started in her direction. She answered with a peal of laughter. It was ringing loudly like in waking life. "I'd like to reward your patience with something," saying that she floated over the flowers. "Wait, don't leave yet!"I yelled to her. "Come, hold my hand,' she whispered grabbing my arm. The ceiling opened up above us, and we were swimming through fog banks toward a white bed. The closer we got to it the bigger it became. "Do you love me?" Wearing her dress with the small flower pattern she stretched out on the white bedcover. "I want you," I said quietly. She slowly started to get undressed. Her white, pointed breasts popped out, her smooth, hairless crotch came into view as naturally as any exposed part of her body, like an armpit. "Take me into your arms," she drew me closer welding her lips to mine. With a clumsy but unstoppable movement I slipped

100

inside her. She took a quick breath, but then she put her arms around me. She tightened her hold on me until her embrace became unbearably painful and it made me lose consciousness.

"What's wrong with you?" Baldy pulls at my coat sleeve, "We have to get off here."

That day, even though neither of us volunteered for overtime, we still didn't get home before seven, because Saul thought of something important in the last minute; we had to clean up the instant coffee extractor and the attic room that housed it. The two of us struggled for more than an hour to remove the sticky black goo from the stainless-steel funnel, inside and outside. Afterwards it took us a half an hour to clean ourselves, we were so smudged up.

By the time we enter the food store we can hardly stand on our feet, so weak we are with hunger. This time we take care to buy enough for two days, just as a precaution. "Just in case it occurs to you to undertake more drudgery well into the night, because you want to send packages home."

Stepping into the dorm we're greeted by Mathman with the news that he has a letter from his fiancée in Australia. He holds high the business-size letter with two creases and filled with writing from top to bottom where it ends in the cipher XOXOXO.

"What does that mean?"

"How could you be so dumb?" says he, with a sad sigh. "It means kisses and hugs; I kiss you and hug you a thousand times."

I have nothing to add. Instead, I sit with Baldy whose mouth is so full he cannot move his jaws to chew. My stomach feels it holds a cannonball inside. The cold beer hits the spot though. This time we purchased the gold-collared brand. My arms are still aching from lugging them.

Wiseman sits down with us. I offer him a beer, but le looks at me with disdain.

"I do not consume alcohol," he rejects the invitation with great emphasis, "only mineral water. I need all my neurons unharmed. You too would be better off without it. I don't understand why you spend every minute working. Shouldn't you spend all your time in preparation?"

"Preparing for what?"

"For immigration. Do you speak the language of the country you are hoping to move to?"

"I must confess I don't."

"Then what are you waiting for? You drive yourself ragged every day. What are you going to do without any language skills in your new country?"

"As long as I can find work, I must take it. I have no funds available to me like you do. I left a family of three at home. I have to earn money to support them. In any case when winter starts in earnest, I'll have nothing else to do but learn the language."

"It's up to you. But don't complain later I didn't warn you. And in good time."

I certainly don't need this lecture. I'm already, as always, getting ground up by the millstones of doubt. Now I have no desire for anything, not even sleep. I cannot help it but keep thinking of Nina and I'm afraid to fall asleep lest I dream about her again. The same dream.

Only a few days pass, and I find myself outside the mainstream of the Regal community. The smell of money, the sweet smell of success estranges me from the others, it segregates me, turns me into someone I cannot recognize. Someone who seems rigid, repulsive, alien.

* * * *

Baldy's been in good mood for the past few days. Now I've found out why. According to the unwritten regulation governing the illegal labor market, the coffee factory can only employ Regal residents – or any other illegal aliens - for a one-week stretch at a time.

"Do you hate this outfit that much?" I ask as we're headed toward a tractor trailer waiting to be unloaded.

"I've had it of all this. And you, too," and he gives me sharp look. "At least now I won't have to worry about you signing up for overtime work. You've gone nuts, this demented workload is equal to suicide."

"Did you know we were going to get sacked after one week?"

"Yes, thank heavens."

"Why didn't you pass that on to me?"

"So that you take on even more extra work?"

After lunch Julia comes to the loading area. For a few minutes she just stands there watching us work.

"I need one pair of extra hands in the night shift."

There are six of us working there, but none speaks up.

"I'll do it!" I yell out.

"Come to my office at five," she turns to me without looking at me.

Baldy makes a grimace at me. He needs to say no more.

We keep on trucking.

If indeed this is my last day here, might as well take full advantage of it. Who knows when they are going to start hiring again in the vineyards again, I try to sooth my overwrought nerves and avoid Baldy's eyes.

It's five past five when I report in Julia's office. First thing she does she has me change from a blue to a white work coat which is a little longer and looser. But we are already stepping into the packing area. The packing machine is run by a man and two girls. With me, a team of four. My job is to catch the freshly packed 250-gram bags coming down the assembly line and place them in a carton box. When it fills up, I seal it with packing tape and put it on a palette. The job description allows for relief by one of the girls when I cannot keep up with the assembly line.

The minutes of the first hour seem to crawl compared to the bags that come shooting down fast and furious. I can't find a comfortable position to catch five or six bags at a time and stack them in the box before I have to reach for the new ones inexorably coming toward me. The devilish pace wears me out, making me feel helpless. When I can stand it no longer I ask for relief in the person of the girl working closest to me, watching over the vacuum sealing of the bags, while I go to the washroom. I splash cold water on my face, rub it to bring it back to life. I do a few knee-bends, swing my arms, roll my head and go back to work.

"Where've you been all this time?" the girls screams at me. "We almost had to stop the assembly line because of you. One of the bags got caught in the feeder and there was no one here to remove it."

No point answering her. I resume my position at the end of the line. That's when I discover a large number of bags on the floor. I don't know what to grab first. The girl who didn't bother substituting for me while I was out now walks away from the problem, leaving me alone. There's no way out, I have to serve the assembly line first of all. I'll take care of the neglected bags during coffee break. But we get no coffee break. Julia ordered that we finish processing the coffee waiting for us nonstop; no one is to go home before then.

At midnight I begin to feel nauseous, close to fainting. My arms and back have gone numb.

The girl notices I'm reeling and sends me to the washroom. I put my head under the cold-water faucet. My shirt, too, gets a soaking, but I seem to regain my strength in spite of my deadly pallor and bloodshot eyes.

At three in the morning she brings me strong coffee and puts it on a box.

"If all goes well, we may finish by four," she tries to outshout the rumbling of the machine.

Something about what she says gets to me, and I start laughing. I can't help it, I keep laughing while the shiny coffee bags keep falling off the assembly line, making a sizable mound on the floor. The bigger the pile gets the harder, the more hysterically I laugh.

"You gone mad?" the girl screams and starts to collect the neat, boxy-looking coffee bags in my place.

I just continue laughing steadily, unable to stop.

After that there's nothing but the buzzing and rattling of the machines, the rhythmic bending down, colors washing into one another at my feet and that one overriding thought: to sleep, sleep and sleep. Doesn't matter where or how, but I've got to sleep.

I still don't know how I got back to the Regal; all I recall is waking up as if from a faint by my bunk and falling into bed fully clothed. I have no strength to undress. I just turn over and pull the blanket over my face.

* * * *

"If you don't keep your eyes on those lights," the old man points toward a line of bright pinpricks in the dark, still far away, "you'll get off the path going across the border and you'll double back to where you started. Make a good note of this. See those lights over there? Keep them always in your sight, that's what you have to aim at."

Rain water is running down the sleeve of his jacket. He doesn't shake the raindrops off even though they've soaked through the fabric. I can't actually see it but figure it must be like mine. I can feel the horrifying coldness of the rain seeping through my light linen jacket.

The old man turns to get back into the car without a farewell. I'd like to crawl back to the back seat, but I can't make a move. I'm just standing there, rooted to the ground.

Can't take a step forward or back.

In the faint light of the dashboard the outlines of the old man's stolid face stand out. That's the last I see of him. However, the thing that occupies my mind is not that, but with obsessive curiosity I wonder what's going through his mind. If anything at all.

The driver lets the engine growl softly as he makes a K turn on the narrow dirt road like a ghost, only a step away from the spot that holds me by my newly sprung roots.

The arc of a light beam leaps out of the dark and splits the dark sky in half. It lights up the black-clad terrain. Without even thinking about it, I dive into the cornfield. I don't even wonder how I'd suddenly regained my mobility.

I crouch among the cornstalks. I have sore muscles in my legs and my feet are developing blisters. Yet I haven't taken more than ten steps. It's time to get moving.

The lightning bolts quickly follow one another, releasing deafening thunderclaps from the night sky. The dance of the fireworks slowly moves on, but the symphony of the sky stays on molto crescendo.

How can anyone see me in the midst of this storm? My nerves settle down slowly. Ready to go.

But the tall cornstalks obstruct my vision of the lights I am to keep in my sight.

How am I going to find my way to freedom?

I don't even notice it when my blood circulation gets back to normal and my calves regain their strength.

At long last, at the edge of the cornfield, the lights the old man pointed out gradually come into my view again. The darkness separating me from them is now sinking back into silence. I make my way in that direction whatever it is I have to wade through. Wet corn is replaced by wet branches, but they keep snapping at me all the same.

They hurt only my thoughts, not my body.

I do not stray from my direction.

Light enters my world, but it remains swaying above me. At the same time my ears recognize the usual hullabaloo, the sounds of the Regal Babel. I refuse to open my eyes. I lack the will power. But I am becoming fully aware and cognizant of my surroundings.

"I'm okay," the thought flashes through my mind. "Okay."

I feel a hand on my shoulder.

"I'd thought you'd never get home. You passed out for real, didn't you? Did you need this?" Baldy addresses me from behind, waiting for me to turn over. "It was madness what you did, sheer madness."

"Let me sleep some more. We'll talk later," I pull the blanket over my face.

* * * *

The cathartic drama of dawn is playing itself out in front of my half-open eyes, the dance of breath-light shadows in the capacious distance beyond the windows. Hesitant imagination is caught in the wrinkles of fresh light now pushing a cart filled with unforeseeable events.

I'm on the lookout for the first gleam of daylight in order to account for what I'm incapable of resurrecting from the quagmire of memory.

I'm keeping pace with the moment.

The moment never hurries.

Neither do I.

The realization that I am at liberty this morning, I have no place to rush, steals inordinate amount of relief into my heart along with a feeling of confidence.

Today I am not reporting at the coffee roasting plant for work but visiting there to collect my wages.

In my mind I'm going over the figures and how big a package I can send home from the final tally.

It's an exercise that catapults me from inner peace to palpable happiness.

It is not worry that keeps me tossing and turning but being well-rested, and I am careful not to disturb the others whose bunk is attached to the same steel frame. I don't remember waking up as early and in such good spirits in the Regal ever since my arrival.

Finally, it's time to go out to the washroom. I take a hot shower, but my clothes are rather smelly. The pair of blue jeans I have is the only one, and I don't have a choice, but I do have a clean shirt in reserve in my brown bag. I'll have to buy decent clothes, at least enough for a change, but that'll have to wait. The food package should come first,

To my great surprise Baldy is quite effusive, greeting me with hearty Good Morning. As if a twin of his had switched places with him.

107

"The cashier opens at nine. I figure if we leave here at half past, we should be there in plenty of time," he says guessing and foiling my forthcoming question.

On the way I fill him in on the events of the night shift. I don't leave out the fact I still don't remember how I got back to the Regal.

"A sticky situation," Baldy shakes his head. "It's not impossible Julia might refuse to compensate you for last night."

He could be turning a knife in my heart.

"And why should she? Didn't I work the whole eight hours?"

"What if she docks your pay for the damages you caused?"

"Damages?"

"Didn't you say the coffee packages were falling off the assembly line like ripe fruit from a tree?"

Baldy succeeds in planting the seeds of doubt in my mind; I feel defeated by anxiety. I can entertain no other notion in my mind except that I'll be getting gypped, getting a whole lot less than I've been hoping for.

There are three trucks parked by the loading docks. The forklifts are not too far behind. I watch their circling motion dispassionately but also relieved. They are no longer part of my life. They are already history to me, maybe not ancient but definitely in the past. I regard them as the painful afterglow of my tribulations.

There are only the two of us waiting at the cashier's window. Baldy steps up first. He gives his name. Signs the time sheet. Collects the banknotes counted out into his hand.

It's my turn.

My hands are shaking. I watch the bills of one hundred denomination as they sidle up against one another.

We say good-bye.

In the corridor we stop to count the bills again.

"They over-payed me." Baldy lets his breath out with a long hiss. "How about you? Did they hold back the nightshift pay?"

"I don't know yet. Wait, let me count the wad again. No, they did not hold back anything, just the contrary. I got two hundred more than supposed to! How do you like that? Finally, something good's happening to us!"

"We have to turn back. They must've made a mistake," Baldy puts his hand on the door jamb.

"I'm going exactly nowhere! If they made a mistake, it was their mistake. We worked hard for every penny of it," I try brushing his hand off the door. "Let's take the money and run!" Nothing can sour my good mood now, not even the question: What should make me happier, the fact that they miscalculated the wages or that they chose not to impose a penalty for what happened late at night.

At the front exit we run into Julia.

"Well, young man, have you rested up yet?" she looks and sounds genuinely friendly this time.

"Why? You have more work for us?" I cannot help but take advantage of the situation and make fun of it, without even thinking.

"When we do, I'll send for you," she smiles at my eagerness. "You fellows did a good job, very handy you are, both of you. Saul and I decided to give tangible sign of our appreciation by topping off your pay by a couples of hundred. Okay, fellows, best of luck to you." She turns around and hurries toward the stockroom.

If the day starts out well one cannot help but worry that it will end badly. That's what flashes across my mind as we amble out of the factory site toward the tram stop.

Our destination is the food store. Baldy is increasingly irritable; he claims it's been an hour since I started staring at the shelves and my basket I still empty. Yes, it's time I'd stopped weighing the advantage of every item over every another, and time to make a few hard decisions. I quickly assemble the contents of the package, concentrating only on essentials.

All set to go.

On a recommendation from Whiskers I visit a second-hand clothing store in the afternoon a few blocks away from the Regal. I pick out two pants and three shirts, but the last minute I add to the cart a checkered gray suit hanging in front of my eyes. I even try on the last item, just to be safe.

It fits me great.

"But you need a topcoat, too, with that," the sales clerk teases me. He casts the gleam of his black eyes at me. A devilish smile curls the corners of his mouth.

A quick accounting of the money spent so far yields favorable results.

"Fine, please, show me something."

Next, I'm on my way back to the Regal.

Baldy's eyes open wide when he sees me in my new suit in the middle of the dorm where I model my acquisitions for the opinion of my fellow inmates.

"All you need is a new pair of shoes and you'll be outfitted like a real gentleman." He feels the fabric of my suit.

"Fresh out of cash. Maybe if I get work again."

"Yeah, work again. I'll see what I can do about it," he adds laconically.

Wiseman draws closer, too. He examines my outfit with a deprecating grimace.

"So you waste your hard-earned money on new clothes, instead of studying the language and getting ready for your new country."

"But none of these are new, they were almost free in the rummage store."

"They sure look like it," he walks away before I can give him a dirty look.

Maybe I'd better put an end to this impromptu fashion show, I decide and get back into my old clothes. Just as I finish changing Mathman walks in.

"Let's pay a visit to Teenie and let her treat us to coffee," he proposes.

After a full day's rest, it feels good to stretch my legs.

At the last minute, Whiskers joins us too.

We're ambling on the gravel path of the park toward the female residence.

The sun sits on the hillcrest before us as if stuck up there and nothing is ever going to move it from its perch.

In the air a tousled faced autumn is riding the winds among bushes weighted down with nostalgia.

In my nose I detect the scent given off by the passage of time.

"Can I rent your jalopy for the evening?" asks Mathman when the white car catches his eye from behind a screen of bare trees.

"It's yours, screw it. We had fun last night, Blondie and me, screw it," Whiskers is blustering magnanimously.

We find Teenie lying on top of her bed. She's fully dressed, even kept her shoes on like someone who's always on call and expecting the unexpected.

Nina is sitting at the larger table in the middle of the dorm, busy writing on a sheet of paper.

Seeing me she mellows into a pale smile. Gorgeous, I observe to myself, she's even prettier than she was in my dream.

But only the real Nina can make the dream come true, it's no use superimposing the dream over reality, marble breasts and her inviting crotch over the dress she has on.

She becomes embarrassed.

Stands up.

"You fellows want coffee," she says closing her eyes and taking hold of the half-filled sheet of paper.

"Stay still," I step closer to her and take hold of her hand.

Teenie jumps up from the bed.

"Hi, fellows. I was only taking a siesta. Tonight I have to go in early. There's a party this afternoon; they'll tear the place apart by the time I get in." She leaves the room with the preserve jar in her hand.

Mathman is busy talking to Whiskers; it seems I'm alone with Nina. I sit down next to her.

111

"I want you," I tell her sotto voce, seeking her gaze with my eyes.

"It won't work. I'm already spoken for. My fiancé is waiting for me in the States."

"And in the meantime?"

"Nothing."

"I had a dream about you the other night."

"And what? How was I?"

"Wonderful. And…"

"And what?"

"We made love."

"That's how you got the idea to go to bed with me?"

"It only confirmed my feelings for you."

"But you're married with two kids. Have you forgotten them?"

"This has nothing to do with them."

"If you're lonely, I don't think I am the medicine for your problem." Nina finally turns to face me directly.

Mathman drinks up his coffee and retreats to a corner with Teenie in tow. In a few minutes they say good bye and leave the room.

"What's happening?" I look at Whiskers.

"Nothing, screw it. They're off to have a quickie, screw it. Didn't you hear it? Teenie has to go to work early tonight."

Blondie doesn't get home until we're ready to leave.

"Hi everybody," she says on her way to her bed. "I'm very tired tonight."

And it shows; her face is especially pale.

* * * *

Later that night I'm awakened by hollers of demented intensity. By the time I am alert enough to see what's going on, Curly is fully engaged in a fight with two of his younger dormitory mates, the same ones he had been altercating with a few days earlier.

"Just look at yourself, you old turd, look what's become of you." One of his opponents is baiting him while the other delivers a powerful whack to his back. Curly is thrashing the air with his arms, his eyes vacuous, his face distorted by some animal passion.

"Rip out his liver!" hollers the barber coming to the aid of his friends.

Not that they need any help. The drunk is soon on the floor, and the others are on top of him pummeling him with their fists wherever they can reach him until, out of breath, they get up, leaving the loser alone.

Curly is down but not out yet, he keeps rolling on the floor emitting inarticulate whimpers. A pitiful sight, in anyone's eyes.

"He asked for it," says Wiseman. "I was here, I saw what happened. He was the one who started it, he tore into the boys, calling them all kinds of names."

As always, it's their better chances at getting accepted as immigrants that infuriates Curly against the younger men. He is more than twenty years older and yet can't seem to understand the selection process used by the receiving countries with regard to prospective immigrants; the combination of need and the evaluation system, not to speak of the message implicit in the way they go about the administration of the process. Perhaps Madam Olga's definition describes it best; it's simply a modern version of a slave market. Curly cannot understand this world and takes refuge in the netherworld of alcohol every time his mind is overwhelmed by waves of bitterness, and he wants to seek revenge on those who appear to reap rewards without earning them, without proving themselves worthy in a level playing field. He keeps blaming groups of others for his lack of success; he can't understand the struggle here is between lone wolves. Everyone here has to prove himself as an individual, alone; group tactics in this situation do not apply.

I can understand what's been eating on Curly's mind better than he does; his trouble is he keeps putting it in the wrong words. He cannot face the simple truth of the same questions that have been bothering everyone, including me: Will I succeed as an immigrant in a strange new country? Will I ever be admitted there? Do I meet the criteria? Can I add up enough points in my favor to get a passing score?

Finding a permanent home country is the foremost issue on every Regal resident's mind, even though few words are wasted on it. The uncertainty of our position here, the possibility of never moving beyond here slowly turns into fear, the horror of the end; the longing for self-fulfillment keeps everyone in a constant state of tension, ready to grab the other fellow's throat at the slightest provocation.

A gaunt older gentleman, camped out in a corner bunk, has attracted my attention in the past. His calm demeanor is in pleasant contrast to his environment. Whenever it comes to fisticuffs, he withdraws to his hammock without a word. He watches events unfold from that vantage point. But now he reacts differently to Curly's whimpers and convulsions on the floor. He gets up from the bunk and steps over to Curly. Leans over him, their faces almost touching.

"Get up, now!" he orders Curly.

The other continues to wiggle and whimper on the floor, as if tortured by pain or under the influence of recreational drugs.

"You've brought me shame! Can't you hear me? Get back on your feet at once!" the gaunt dark man, usually so reticent, now yells at his protégé.

The man on the floor seems to sober up for a moment and tones down his whimpers to a chant. He struggles to his feet. He loses his balance several times, until he can no longer compensate, but as soon as he falls on the floor, he struggles up again.

The fragility of every move he makes is pitiful and at the same time laughable. The grotesque pirouettes dissolve the drama of the situation into embarrassment. By now everyone seems to feel sorry for Curly and watch his progress with empathy.

"Come on, I'll help you," his friend puts an arm around Curly's waist. "How many times I've asked you not provoke

114

the boys, not to pick on them. They never did anything to hurt you. Why keep picking on them? Lie down, I'll pull up your blanket," he says with pity while trying to keep both of them from falling until they get to the bunk.

The boys are standing with the barber, watching the awkward maneuvers of the drunk and his friend. The youngest among them spits on the floor.

"Pests," he hisses between his teeth.

But most people just turn away in silence.

I cannot fall asleep. My thoughts inevitably travel back home. It's an emotional handhold, a spiritual crutch that helps me over the rough terrain of reality.

Tomorrow it's back into the fray.

* * * *

Can we start something all over again even if it never existed in the first place? Or it existed all right but not the way it actually came about, because memory alters everything once it's taken place. Changes its form, sprinkles time powder of different scent on it so that I cannot, even by my sense of smell, recognize something that was once mine. The reality of time always deceives my consciousness, always fools me and makes it impossible for me to recognize the fact that everything is a resurgence of something that existed before. But if the *is* of today is not the recurrence of the *was* of yesterday, then what...? I recall the days in the coffee roasting plant, when I was chosen and rewarded because my work was valued and so was my strength and willpower. Was that merely the happy coincidence of accidental events?

*

It's been over an hour, and there are ten of us still standing in the plaza in front of the Regal.

The demand is weak in the labor market today.

"How did it go yesterday? Was it as bad as today?" I ask one of those stomping their feet near me.

"Only three got hired," says the man before taking a long drag on the umpteenth cigarette of the day. He drops the butt on the edge of the sidewalk, squashes it under his heel while letting the smoke out and speaking at the same time. "If, in fact, yesterday's market performed three hundred percent better than today's."

When it gets past eleven, I give up. No point waiting around any longer. But it hurts to admit failure, I'm reluctant to return to the Regal having been warned this morning by Baldy it was useless looking for work today, I'd better stay in my room and get some rest or write home. I don't relish the thought of proving him right.

I head for the food store. I purchase sweets, coffee, and other little Christmas presents for my sons. I figure it should take about five weeks for the package to get there, even considering the fact that we're not yet into the rush of the holiday season.

It comes to six kilos. The postage costs more than the contents. But in my mind's eye I can just see how happy they're going to be opening the package from abroad, from dad.

The image fills me too with happiness.

I get back to the Regal early afternoon. Baldy's resting, stretched out on his bed. Seeing me, he gives me a hearty greeting. To my surprise he puts aside fiendish glee even though I'm sure he heard about this morning's unsuccessful job market from the other would-be day-workers who were out there with me without getting hired.

"Two of the young ones got their immigration permits today. They'll soon be flying to Canada!" He's so full of excitement; it's as if he were talking about his own travel plans.

So far I've had no reason to check or even look for the immigration list. Baldy tells me it's posted on the same bulletin board where mail recipients are notified.

"Positively astounding how many have received entrance visas," I tell Baldy on my return from the bulletin board. "Next week four groups are scheduled for the US, one to Australia, and two to Canada."

"Looks like they've speeded up the pace of moving people out of here for Christmas." He places both hands under his pate. "Watch the crowds gather in the ground floor dormitories tomorrow. That's where they put up those scheduled to travel, not only from the Regal but from the outlying camps and converted resorts. They will be transported by buses to the airport Monday morning."

I feel excitement coursing through my whole being. As if I was already among the lucky ones. I wonder how I am going to feel when the sole aim of my stranded existence here comes into my view, when the possibility of that almost mythical freedom finally knocks on my door, when my screwed-up life takes a new tack and the borders suddenly open up before me? Will I be ready to stretch out in my hard-won freedom, laying out on the raft of imagination and sailing across seas and oceans, fully cognizant of the dangers and tribulations ahead?

Could the whole thing be as simple as that?

Or will I cave in under the weight of all the imponderables?

* * * *

I wake up well-rested.

It's very quiet around me.

Dawn arrives unobserved in a scarlet chariot.

It blinks its lights.

I'm waiting for someone among my friends to get up, but everyone's asleep.

This minute too refuses to pass.

* * * *

Wiseman and I meet up in the ground floor lobby. He's overawed by the sight of the crowd congregating there. He seems to seek his own pleasure in their joy, his own fate in theirs. It's a cavalcade, a holiday, a massing of troops for

117

inspection. It's a rally of families, men, women, young and old, all on a display of great significance.

Till tomorrow this place will be ruled by nothing else but joy and unselfconscious merriment. The delirium of high spirits is infectious, and we catch it, too. We're in it up to our ears, and yet we stand outside this overflowing sentiment.

"…did you bring water? can't you even do that much?… Watch the kid, I'll run out to the washroom… any message for Anna?… don't you worry about it, it's nothing… you were in love? and now you confess it… did you see Miki's dumbstruck mug, he kept saying we'd never amount to anything… don't make the bed there, take the one next to it… please, pay attention for once, I've been telling you for days… I clasped his hand as if never to let go of it again… no, he's not going to follow us, who knows what's going to become of the poor thing here… you could've waited till tomorrow with this… my god, where's that child again? That's all I asked of you, watch him while I was in the washroom… yes, I've written to her but received no answer… What time is your flight?… I told the proprietor that was it, we were finished… the family back home?… he was begging my forgiveness, but what for… look, it was all right while it lasted, you two hopped into bed together, now it's time to forget it… I could beat the shit out of his ugly mug, you thinking he was making a fool of me… as soon as I get there I'll call you, I've got your number in my address book… they set out a full table, threw a real party, it's a once in a lifetime move… don't ask me how I felt, that rotten beast ruined my life… Where's the kid?… the starter engine kept grinding away, but nothing, give it to someone, make a present of it… Well, not even half of the story is true, that pixie slut… Where have you been dear child, didn't mom ask you to stay close, she's going to cry her eyes out if you get lost… there was no need to just let him keep it, the hell with him… keep quiet for a minute, I can't hear a word of what you're saying, bring me my stockings… imagine that, just now he shows up, what am I going to do…"

I'm enthralled by all this hurry-up-and-wait activity. It's as if I were loitering back at the outdoor market set up in the town square, listening to the dialogues of the vendors arriving at dawn. When my father sent me as a child out there early to reserve a spot for him, I got up a half an hour earlier just so I could witness this unique show, this daily stage production. I understood very little of what I heard, but I enjoyed being in the middle of all the commotion. To that child it was an exhilarating experience. There was so much to spy on, overhear, and to puzzle over.

Among these peasant women turned busy vendors for the market day.

All I had to do was stand still and pass the time.

It was a simple task to find a premium space and hold it for my dad until he got there with sausages, ham and bacon – delicacies, as he called them - which he later hawked aggressively to the passersby.

He was truly convinced that his merchandise was superior to any other in the whole city. This conviction made him an especially enthusiastic salesman.

Often he took his own spiel to heart and he got emotional almost as if a prophet was speaking through him, not a hapless and embittered man, constantly mired in financial distress.

"The day will come when we are among them," Wiseman opens his arms toward the crowd. "Unusually large group. Never seen so many emigrants at one time," and then he turns to me with a face composed for more serious matters. "I have a bone to pick with you. Instead of hitting the language books you're wasting your time on trivia."

"Why can't you understand I don't have the luxury of free time like you! There's a basic existential difference between us. And not just you and me. Take Mathman, for instance. His girlfriend in Australia invites him to join her and get married. What does he do? He buys a train ticket, packs a suitcase, mortally insults his wife, ignores his hysterically sobbing daughter, goes out to the train station and takes a seat in a first class compartment. Arrives in this so-called Free World and takes a taxi to the Regal. He marches into the holding tank with a pack full of food, and when he walks out, his first order of business is to bed down Teenie. In the meantime, another girlfriend of his shows up and they spend two nights screwing in a four-star hotel, all expenses paid by the girl. After that he ambles back to the Regal with a look of innocence to go on screwing Teenie, the gal of his dreams, to whom he pledges eternal love."

"You're suffering from sexual frustration."

"Yes, from that too! I've been courting Nina, trying to get her to lie down for me, and guess what she says: 'Sorry, I'm engaged. My fiancé is waiting for me in the US'. So who's the fool?"

"Obvious."

"Am I really such an idiot?"

"Perhaps not, only unlucky, for sure."

"It's easy for you to talk. You take a walk to the washroom and jerk off at your leisure. Costs you nothing, hardly any effort at all. Certainly no heartache, no desire, no dreams."

"A physiological necessity. That's what it's called."

"Call it what you will. I've had it up to here with you. You kill the little spirit that's still left in me. You play the guru who knows it all. You tell me what to do when I arrive in my new home country. My god, where is it yet, my new homeland! Light years away from here. I can't even find the old one, and yet it was still here yesterday, in my mind, my destiny, my soul, in my despondent thoughts."

"Let me know when you calm down and come to your senses."

Wiseman turns on his heels and leaves me there alone, in the middle of the cavalcade, the celebrating multitudes.

Where the clock of the future spins quiet minutes into nothingness.

* * * *

120

I'm about to head back to the dorm.

"Do you know Father Petri?" Blondie comes up to me. By her side is a balding man of average height smiling at me.

"Laudatur Jesus Christi, Father."

"In aeternam, amen. How long have you been here?" he examines me with cold, piercing eyes that belie his smile.

"A few weeks."

"No wonder we haven't met yet."

"I'm not exactly a regular church-goer either."

"You aren't? And why not?" he looks at me with genuine disapproval.

"In my childhood I used to go to mass with my great-grandmother. After she'd taken to her bed, I stopped. And never resumed. You know, worship was very much discouraged by the regime."

"Here's your chance to make a new start. I say mass every Sunday at ten in the morning at the Regal. The chapel is on this floor to the left, at the end of the corridor. Come a little earlier so that we get better acquainted."

"I'll do my best to be there," I bow my head like someone with much to atone for.

We say goodbyes shortly.

Blondie lingers.

"What's got into you?" I turn to her.

"A nice man. He tries to help everyone. You too may need some kind of help."

"Sure, sure, but first I'll have to attend mass."

"I suggest you do. The old man remembers everyone he meets and if you fail to show up for mass he'll have you tracked down and brought to him. You'll benefit from his influence. He works closely with the registration office. If you attend mass, that counts for good behavior, extra brownie points."

"How long have you been attending his masses?"

"Ever since I arrived. At first I thought it was a joke, this religious nonsense. But on one occasion the ceremony

121

reminded me of my mother I lost when I was fourteen. From then on I've always found peace of mind in the chapel."

"What ailed your mother?"

"She was a heavy drinker. It got to her liver. You know the story. One morning I found her lying on the floor, near the table. I nudged her, but she did not respond. My dad had been hit by a bus a year earlier. He was still alive when they got him to the hospital. The doctor said the operation was successful, but the heart could not take it. It just quit."

"And who raised you?"

"There was no one in the big family willing to take me in. They all had their own problems, and I ended up in an institution. An orphanage – to tell the truth," she poked me with an elbow, furrowing her brows.

"You've never mentioned these things."

"You expect me to stand on the street corner and trumpet it to the whole world? If you want to know, Teenie has the same background. Now you know everything."

"Not everything, but certainly more about you. But you two will be moving on soon, won't you?"

"So far it's open to question. The prospective countries do not favor single women."

"Is that so?"

"So that means I should get married. A married couple gets the green light immediately."

"What does Whiskers say about that?"

"He's all for it. He too is single."

"That's one way to solve that problem," I keep the conversation going, but my mind is elsewhere. We both fall silent, lost in our own thoughts. "Let's make coffee," I finally suggest, just so that we get off the subject.

* * * *

Having climbed the stairs to the second floor I encounter a small group of idlers staring into Dorm No. 8 through the open door. I spy the gleam of beer bottles inside. Curiosity draws me closer. In the middle of the ten-bed room five young men are singing softly and dancing, arms linked. Although they're stripped to shirtsleeves, they have perspiration beading their foreheads. Apparently unaware of their surroundings they're concentrating on the steps they keep varying, improvising. Their legs rhythmically rise and dip and then again fly up into the air like the wings of a cliff-dwelling eagle; then the mood changes, the dance becomes slower and the song takes on an elegiac tone.

I discover a few familiar faces among the spectators. For example, the skinheads in dark costumes who so rudely ejected me from their room when I entered by accident a few days earlier. One of them has a highly polished huge chain link in his hand while one of his associates wields a thick metal rod. Slapping their trouser legs, they keep up with the rhythm. A grin of frightening disgust sits on their faces.

The nostalgic folk dance of the boys is suddenly disrupted. One of their own runs in, out of breath, telling them to report some place immediately for a roll call. The spectators disperse.

"Do you know the boys in number 8?" I ask Baldy as soon as I enter my dorm.

"Yeah, I've heard about them. They're all right. In fact I'm quite chummy with one of them. They're from the country. They work at a construction site not far from here. What about them?"

"Nothing, I just saw them dancing."

"They must be happy."

"Six of them, if I got it right, will be flying to Canada next Thursday."

"Yes, I know. My god, they too are moving on."

"Soon it should be our turn. Isn't that right?"

Baldy stares at the floor, silent.

I leave him to his thoughts.

* * * *

123

The Regal has a sizable park, but a resident can appreciate it only when he has nothing urgent to do. The park must be enjoyed at leisure; it's much bigger than it seems at first sight.

Today I explore the parts behind the buildings. My view is obstructed by high concrete walls, no matter which way I look. Beyond them though snowcaps sparkle like fish scales in sunlight.

In my painful loneliness, my thoughts flock back home. I wonder if they've received my letter yet. If I don't get an answer by next week, I'll have to give them a call. But why have I let so much time pass without even thinking of that? What am I waiting for?

* * * *

The next morning, I wake up to another bout of chest pain. I can hardly breathe, the pressure inside is so overpowering. The medication! Quick, where is it? Luckily there's plenty of it left. The hard work in the coffee packaging plant cured me of my psychological or psychosomatic "illness", and I stopped taking the medication.

However, an hour goes by, and I don't feel any better. I call out to Baldy. He advises me to lie flat on the bed and rest. "Work can wait, you'll pick it up again tomorrow."

I can't figure him out. In the beginning he was the one who pushed me into work.

But I choose not to debate the issue.

Best give in to him.

The more I think about it, the better I feel. Whether it's the medication or the rest, it's hard to tell. In a half an hour the stabbing chest pain ceases.

Without saying anything to anyone I get myself together and slip out the door.

The ground floor corridor is full of people, those scheduled to resettle in distant lands. There seem to be even more of them today than yesterday.

Outside in a corner of the courtyard there are three white buses parked by the pedestrian island.

The sight intoxicates me. It is with bitter longing that I watch the faces bathed in elation, I feel the tension vibrate in the air, I smell the special scent of happiness.

The quiver.

Slowly, majestically, one of the buses pulls up to the entrance, stops, gives a wheeze and opens a door.

Let me remember this morning, I tell myself, putting the experience in storage for future use. For the time when I'll be climbing into the bus, delirious with a wish fulfilled. Now, I cannot afford to get emotional, I must go and take my place in the shop window of the day-workers.

Just as soon as I'm out there, a large, old-model car comes to a halt next to me.

"You got a driver's license?" And older gent leans out the window.

"Yes, but I don't drive commercial vehicles."

"No need. But it's a two-week job. Are you good for it?"

"What kind of work?"

"Interior renovation of an apartment. You accept it?"

"Yes."

"We need one more. Your friend?"

"If you can wait ten minutes, I'll get him."

"Good. I'll be waiting on the corner."

Baldy's mad. Why in hell work for peanuts all the time? But then he gets ready, and we're on our way, back to our new employer.

It takes about an hour before we park in front of a tidy one and a half story home. The old man hurries to open the gate and leads us to the back of the yard, to a lemon-yellow station wagon. He swings open the back hatch and shows us what tools to pack into the luggage compartment. Baldy and I get to work loading the vehicle.

The boss comes back wearing a blue overall. He keeps nodding, looking satisfied.

"Put that tin wheelbarrow on the top," he points to a rusty old thing.

We don't care, we don't opine, we do as we're told. The last minute he remembers the cement. We stuff three bags in the back.

"All set, let's go," he gives the order.

I sit down behind the wheel. I adjust the back view mirrors and turn the ignition key. Nothing. I try again. Nothing.

"Must be the battery's down," he gets out and runs into the shack.

"Come you men, here's the other battery, help me with it."

That thing is bulky, weighs a ton. The two of us can barely manage. Out with the old, in comes the new. Now we're all set.

I turn the key again. The old jalopy shakes like hell. I step on the gas letting the engine rev up.

"No need to rev the engine. It can start cold. But watch out, the second gear doesn't engage. You have to speed up in first and then put it directly in third. Don't forget, otherwise the engine will stall."

I acknowledge the instructions and get moving. Still in first gear, still in the yard, the cold engine shakes itself to a halt.

The old man's nervous as hell.

Starts yelling.

Waving his arms.

Sputtering a mile a minute.

Making a big thing of everything.

Blaming me.

Finally, we make it out to the highway. It's already ten a.m., but in the four forward lanes the traffic is still barely crawling. It takes us fifteen minutes to finally get into a lane. Suddenly the cars ahead of us start moving. The old man watches every move I make, to see if I follow his instructions: get moving in first, let the engine rev up, then put it in third, fourth, and back to first when another jam develops.

Actually, it's in neutral, we're standing still.

Bang! And crack, followed by an earthquake or a quake that loosens every part of the old jalopy. Bucket and trowels fly from the luggage compartment into the passenger seats.

Baldy holds his head, begging for help.

The crash knocks the steering wheel out of my hands.

The old man hollers, it was my fault, he told me to put it in first then directly into third! I didn't shift according to instructions!

Total chaos.

Then silence.

Even if only for a few seconds but I lost consciousness, because the next thing I know I am the only one sitting in the car.

The boss and Baldy are looking over the car. Standing next to them is a stranger, a man, a new character in the unfolding drama, most likely the driver of the car that ran into us.

From the mirror it looks like to me he's explaining something, trying to calm down the others.

I extricate myself from the car.

"It was your fault, yours alone, because you didn't..." the old man screams at me.

"Why?" I ask, not hiding my shock. "He ran into us from the back, he rear-ended us when we had to stop. Why blame me?"

The other driver waves his hands horizontally, asking for silence.

"It was inattention on my part. Sorry about it. Let's just exchange all the information and my insurance company will pay for your damages," saying that he looks at our car and falls into convulsions of laughter.

"What's so funny?" the old man snorts.

"Nothing, nothing, only that..." the other driver shrugs and continues writing down the relevant data.

In the meantime the police arrive.

The commotion around us intensifies and expands.

Behind us a line of motionless cars standing as far back as the eye can see.

The other driver assures the police that there were no injuries, only material damage.

The police take down all the info all over again.

Two ambulances show up as well, their emergency lights flash a few more times before they quietly move on.

Slowly the traffic starts moving again.

The other driver signs his report and hands it to the injured party.

The old man looks at it for a while, mumbles something.

"Everything o.k.?" asks the man.

"Yes," says the old man and signs it.

The four of us push the damaged vehicle up to the sidewalk.

Then we're left alone.

Baldy complains of a headache. He claims one of the handles of the wheelbarrow hit him.

"You should see a doctor," I suggest.

I'm a fine one to speak; I don't feel much better either. The left side of my head hit the door frame. Most likely that was the cause of my losing consciousness for a brief period.

"On the whole though we've come out of this accident relatively unscathed. Thank God, the old man didn't get a heart attack on us." I summarize the situation, mostly for myself.

All the way home Baldy keeps quiet. Not a word to me.

In the dorm he goes directly to his bed and lies down.

I too climb to my bed.

Well, it was this kind of a day, I say to myself before falling asleep.

* * * *

"Hop to it! You've got mail!" Mathman comes trumpeting. "Check this out, what my fiancée writes: 'I've picked out a cute little house, only twenty-minute-drive from downtown. In my imagination I've already decorated the three bedrooms, the living room and dining room. The backyard is huge. It's got plenty of room for kids. I can hardly wait to have my arms around you. Your little Mousy, XOXOXOXOXO'"

"Terrific, congratulations," I stutter impatiently, eager to get going.

"Let me show you something else!" he flips the pages. "'And I've found you a job.' What do you say to that?"

"I'll be back in a minute," pushing him out of the way I run out of the room, down the stairs.

My heart is throbbing in my throat. The first letter from home. Are they all right? Did they get the package? No way, it's much too early for that. I only mailed it a couple of days ago. But who knows? In any case, the main thing is I have news of them, and that's what counts. Are the little rascals attending kindergarten? Is grandma okay? Are the authorities still harassing our neighbors on my account? So many questions pop up in my head I don't know which one to anticipate, so haphazard and disconnected they are.

A line of ten or fifteen crowd the small hallway that leads to the postal window. Standing in line is part of the routine here at the Regal and it normally fails to faze me, but here and now the wait seems eternal.

My turn comes, as it must, and I hand over my Regal I.D. card. The officer studies my physiognomy. He's holding my card up to his eyes. Then he turns his back to me. As far as I can see through the small window he's rummaging in an elongated box. Then in another. With the same negative result. Maybe it was a mistake, I had no mail, bitterness bites into my chest already.

Finally, his hand slips through the small opening in the window. It holds a white business size envelope.

"Sign it here," he pokes at the X on the attached tab.

The pen in my right hand, the letter in the left. I catch a glimpse of the Canadian crest in the left upper corner.

My first reaction is a feeling of total devastation. I can't care less what it is if it's not what I need so badly, a word from home. I feel all strength seep out of me.

Nevertheless, I rip open the envelope. I try to concentrate on the text typed on the embossed stationery. At first I'm not sure I'm reading it right; am I reading what's written there or something carved into my mind? Can I believe these words? The message is delivered to my consciousness in drips and dribbles: "After careful consideration of your immigration application The Embassy of Canada invites you for an interview at 10 p.m. on November 11th of this year…"

Consideration… Canada… interview… these are weighty words and yet there they are jumping up and down in front of my yes.

I start running and running. My feet hardly touch the ground.

"Let me see it!" Mathman snatches the sheet of paper out of my hand. "Yes sir, this is it! This is what I, too, am waiting for. Congratulations! Look you fellow refugees…" he waves the letter over his head.

"May I see what you've received?" Baldy ambles over to my bed, his eyes bleary from sleep. "Did you get hold of God's feet?"

He scans the letter, mumbling the words to himself.

"The usual phrases. That's what everybody gets." Placing the letter back in the envelope he adds in a plaintive tone: "Actually, not everybody. I've been waiting for mine for over a month."

"What's the date of your interview?" Mathman grabs the letter again from Baldy this time. "What the hell! It's next week, Tuesday! You're damned lucky!"

Everyone in the room comes over to wish me luck and to take part in the impromptu celebration. Everyone joins the party, except me; the mood of joy somehow cannot find fertile soil in my heavy soul. Why can't I accept the fact that this letter represents an important step in my arduous journey toward freedom and the day when I can see my family again.

"We've got to drink to this!" Mathman shouts across the joyous crowd toward me. "You know what that means! Head for the bootlegger for beer!"

"Get me the gold label!" Baldy reminds me on my way out.

We stay up sipping beer until Curly gets home and starts his usual tirades. When he learns from the others about my

130

invitation to the Canadian Embassy, he winds his way to our table to shake hands and congratulate with his drunken slur: "Good for you, my boy! It's been an honor to know you."

Sleep seems to avoid me though. I feel empty, as if I had been cheated out of something, robbed of something of high value. At the same time, the shape, the size, the scent and the touch of that something totally evades my memory.

All I know about that something I lost is that I miss it like a warm embrace.

* * * *

I wake up soaked in perspiration. The last words of my dream echo in my mind: "Let's land now! Now, I beg of you!"

I close my eyes again and let the images of the dream return.

I'm standing in a telephone booth, dialing an old friend I have not seen for ages. There's no ring after the dial tone, his voice comes on immediately.

"What on earth made you think of me after all these years?" he sounds offended, not inclined to continue the phone conversation.

"I am in great need of your help. Do you still have your pilot's license?"

"Yes, I last flew only a week ago."

"The thing is, I'm standing in a parking lot with my Cessna. I landed only a short distance from here, and I must get back home this evening yet, but I can't, I'm not familiar with the navigation system."

"But how did you manage to get here?"

"The sun was out this morning. I thought I'd take my new plane on a trial run. Once I was in the air, everything seemed to work out for me. No problems. I just kept going, farther and farther, over at least two large cities."

"Did you keep in touch with the air traffic control tower?"

"My radio didn't work. I had a nagging feeling that I was asking for trouble, flying into restricted airspace, and might even get fighter planes sent after me, but nothing happened."

"Sorry, but I don't get it. What's wrong with you?"

"Don't know. Can you help?"

"What is your location now?"

"On a corner. Wait a sec, let me check. At the intersection of Stendhal Boulevard Newton Street."

"Near the produce market?"

"Yes."

"Don't go anywhere. I'll meet you there in twenty minutes."

I hang up the receiver. The parking lot is empty except for my Cessna. Although it's not quite dark yet, the streets are deserted. Suddenly there's thunderstorm. It starts raining, with increasing intensity. I flatten myself against the portal of an apartment house, but I still get splashed on. It's a tremendous downpour, with thunder and lightning.

"Come," my long-neglected friend tugs at my sleeve.

"You're here already?" I ask following him out to the street.

The rain's over as suddenly as it started. The streetlamps go on.

We get into the plane. He takes the controls. The engine roars to life. We're rolling faster and faster in the parking lot.

Soon we're airborne and still climbing. Higher and higher, with fireflies on the run underneath. Suddenly the engine dies and the propeller stops. Silence surrounds us. The darkness of the night builds walls around us.

"Let's land now! Now, I beg of you!" I scream.

We're swimming in black water like the fish of the deep.

* * * *

I open my eyes to shadows chasing one another on the ceiling. A door is slammed with a loud bang.

Baldy comes running to my bunk.

"Horrible, Horrible!"

"What's horrible? Stop frightening me," I sit up.

"In Room Number Eight."

"What happened there?"

"They slaughtered them."

"Slaughtered? Whom?"

"The boys staying there, they slaughtered them."

The words remain undigested in my consciousness.

Baldy's gasping for air.

We run out to the corridor. Our way is blocked by armed police officers. The window's lit up by the whirling red lights of an ambulance.

"Tell me already, what is this all about?" I ask him, quaking like a leaf.

I move forward by a few steps, but a cop waves us back to our room.

Baldy's face is white as a sheet. He collapses into a chair by the table.

"They bludgeoned them to death with steel pipes and heavy chains during the night."

"Who did?"

"The skinheads from the floor above."

Slowly the others come awake. The news spreads in whispers first but then it gets louder.

Hour by hour the horrors of the story take shape. At early dawn someone went to the washroom and happened to see the black-clad skinheads march off. One of them was swinging a reddish steel pipe, another clanging a chain as they were silently sneaking away. It was a ghostly parade, the way they were tiptoeing out single file. When they were gone the witness ventured forth from the washroom, and on the floor of the corridor he came upon some spots that looked suspiciously like drops of blood. All the signs added up to something big. Something very unpleasant. He continued his way down the corridor but then there were no more spots. Backtracking he found them again and they led directly to the door of Room Number Eight. He opened it. Inside the room was dark, the shade on the single window drawn. The door latch was sticky, slippery with some liquid. He found the light switch and turned it on. The light came on a scene that was beyond description. Beyond his worst dreams. He turned around and ran as fast as he could to get the police.

"And you, screw it, in his place, what would you have done, screw it?" Whiskers asked stuttering with shock.

"Nothing. I'd freeze up in a situation like that, that's for sure," said Wiseman. "The only good thing is they didn't have time to kill more than two of them, the rest will recuperate, eventually…"

"Recuperate? The hell they will! One of them had an arm amputated, the other a leg, the third's still in coma, the fourth lost an eye… You want me to go through the list? For God's sake!" Baldy was beside himself. "Who knows if they will ever recuperate."

"How about your friend?" I ask him.

"Maybe he'll pull through. They broke both of his tibias and totally mangled his left arm he used to defend himself."

"Screw it, when are we going to get the hell out of here, screw it? The sooner, the better, screw it! I've had it up to here with the Regal, screw it!" even Whiskers loses his usual equanimity.

"Any arrests yet?" I look to Baldy, the bearer of all tidings.

"Gone, the whole gang. There's nationwide manhunt for them."

"I saw their mug shots on the noontime newscast. What a collection of… of…" For once, words fail Wiseman.

"And just the other day I mistakenly strayed into their cave," I add my bit to myself; there's no need to go into details.

It's an unbearable day. I've lost interest in anything.

It's noon, but I'm not hungry, even though I missed breakfast.

* * * *

It's been over an hour hanging out at the day workers' market, affectionately known as the labor plaza. I'm standing idle here, every portion of my flaccid body aching for the curative effects of strenuous labor. The coffee-packing plant would do me good now.

Handling sacks.

All day long.

All this time, shuffling here on the sidewalk, I've observed only two cars stopping by. The potential employers inside them were very choosy, taking their time to pick out one worker on each occasion.

The rumor is that the grape harvest is over, and I've had my hopes set on a long season. However, this year's crop was way below the usual. The weather was unfavorable in the spring, and later two severe hailstorms damaged the ripening fruits.

I'm toying with the idea that if I don't get hired in another half an hour, I'll walk over to the post office and put in a call to my family. The thought galvanizes me, helps me recover from the horrors of the morning.

And my patience is running out.

"You're wanted in the registration office!" Baldy comes up behind me. "I'm always stuck with the job of tracking you down."

By the time I turn to him it's only his back I see, he's headed back to the Regal.

"I don't understand your resentment, you know I've got to work," I catch up with him as hurries off. "Who's looking for me?"

"Didn't say, just left a message you're wanted in the office."

We part in the courtyard. I search my memory for a possible reason for the summons. Some problems with one of my immigration applications?

The lobby has only a few people standing around. The waiting room is empty. I knock on the door of the office.

"I have the feeling you've forgotten about me," Madam Olga, the administrator, smiles at me.

"Out of the question," I try to assure her, "but I've been working hard in the past two weeks, trying to earn a little cash."

Just now I recall my promise to redecorate the office. To remedy the omission, I take a quick look around to see what needs to be done.

"You received an invitation for an interview from the Canadian Embassy."

"Yes, I did, the day before yesterday," I hasten to explain; perhaps she expected me to report the news. "I was going to come in and discuss it, but I got sidetracked by the unfortunate events..."

"Yes, I'm aware of them," she cuts me short, but then pauses to look at me with a mournful expression. "Yes, what a tragedy. But let me come to the reason I asked you to come in; your papers were returned by the Australian embassy. Look, here. While we filled in every rubric, we need to expand on these two here. They have additional questions to be answered before they can pass judgment on the application. So let's work them out."

"Is it rejected?"

"Not at all. It's only that if at first sight they get the impression the applicant lacks well-founded reason for political asylum they start picking at little details in the application."

"But don't I qualify?"

"Yes, of course, I know you do. Your qualification is well founded, but the Aussies don't want economic refugees. All the details have to be spoon-fed to them. That was why I advised you to apply to Canada as well, just to hedge your bets, you never know. By the time you get an interview with them you'll have had one with the Canadians, you'll be experienced in the ways of these bureaucrats."

"I wouldn't really like to go to Canada."

"A refugee doesn't go where he would like to but where he's accepted. The last time I tried to make that clear to you," she assumes the role of the strict teacher as she looks at me, handing me a pen and clean sheets of paper. "Here, write down the escape and the events leading up to them. That's what they want."

I fill two sheets with my story while Madam Olga immerses herself in her documents.

"All done," I hand over my homework.

She goes over it carefully. She makes minor corrections here and there.

"Essentially this is in the application. But if they wanted a more detailed version, let them have it."

"Everything all right with my Canadian application?"

"Obviously yes. Otherwise they would not have called you in for an interview. If they decide in your favor next week then you may be traveling by December. They've speeded up the immigration process lately. Those who had successful interviews two weeks ago will be sitting in the plane by the end of November."

At this moment, I'm undecided; should I be glad or sad over the news? If Canada accepts me, I'll never have a chance to do an interview with Australia. But what's the difference? The important thing is to get out of this hellhole and move on.

* * * *

I'm fourth in line in the post office for an international telephone call. When I hand over a piece of paper with the country and the number I want to call, the telephone operator takes a second, rather scornful look at me.

I know it's not the number but the country code that gives her pause. And a question. But instead she informs me in a mechanical tone:

"It's not going to be easy. You may have to wait hours to get a line."

"No problem. I have plenty of time. Should get through by closing time, shouldn't we?"

"We'll see. Take a seat," says she beckoning to the person behind me to come forward.

Usually I take some reading material with me if I know I'll have to wait around for a while. But somehow this time I'm here unprepared. Unarmed against boredom.

The situation finds me sitting idle, nothing to occupy me, no one to talk to. But I don't care. The horrendous events of the past few days have caused me so much pain that I'm not really ready for the little joy I hope for on the phone.

"The national phone center of the country you're trying to reach reports that all lines are busy. Do you still wish to wait?" the operator calls out to me from behind her window.

"Absolutely yes!" I even stand up to show my determination.

It's been three hours and still nothing. I'm still just sitting and mulling over my life, past, present and future.

I spend the time reading announcements and advertisements posted on the walls.

I try to avoid speculating about the connection problem.

Dusk has set in.

A tree branch, leaning toward the window, seems to be beckoning to me when the wind shakes it.

"Take booth number two," the telephone operator lady calls out to me.

I quickly turn to the row of booths, but in my haste I can't find number two. They're not numbered in order. There's a number one and next to it number three, but where's number two?

"Hallo, yes, hallo…" nothing but cracks and crackle at the other end. Followed by weighty silence. I keep hitting the hang-up lever. No change, no sound.

"Sorry, I lost the connection. Not my fault though, another call interrupted the connection. You still wish to wait?" my operator's voice comes on in the receiver.

"Yes," I say, but without much conviction.

"Yes or no?"

"Yes!" I reply, this time with renewed determination.

I fall back into my seat again. From that vantage point I watch the streetlamps go on in the ensuing darkness. If I shut my eyes to a very narrow slit the dots of lights multiply and the light pattern they create turns different, too.

Stepping out to the street, I'm assaulted by a cold wind that scours my whole body. Everything around me seems bleak and unfriendly if not downright hostile. The street is deserted. The beams of the railroad crossing gate are standing up straight as if to salute the cold fall weather marching in.

There's not a soul in the courtyard of the Regal. An earlier wind gust had stuck a stray newspaper into a leafless twig on a high branch. The devoted winds have perused it with such vigor that now it is in tatters.

Loneliness is choking my throat.

I head for the women's dormitory building. Most likely the boys too are hanging out there.

Sure enough, the whole gang is there. Sitting around the table; four of them immersed in a card game, with Nina kibitzing Teenie.

"Look who's here. Just a few minutes ago I was telling the boys that soon you too would show your face," says Blondie tossing an ace of diamonds on the pile of cards in the middle of the table.

I take a seat next to Nina, but not only because she happens to have an unclaimed chair next to her.

I take her hand and squeeze it.

"Hi," she turns to me.

"Have you by any chance changed you mind?"

"No," she answers, demonstratively turning away from me.

"What's the matter with you two, screw it, here's the key to the vehicle, go and have a walloping good time, screw it," Whiskers whacks his last card on the table.

Nina gets up and leaves the room.

"Why do you have to be so insensitive?" Blondie cries out.

"Screw it, why go on beating around the bush?"

"True enough, but is this any way to talk?" Teenie picks up the coffee pot and raises it high. "Anyone interested?"

"I am," I raise my hand.

"I figured that."

"I'm chilled to the bone."

"Where have you been? Working"?

"Unfortunately, no. I was passing the time at the post office, trying to make a call to my woman and kids."

"What do you mean, trying?"

"Didn't get past the trying stage," I shrug it off.

"Well, well... What else can you expect from the communist mass communication system and censorship? You don't talk to your family when you want but when they want you to," Mathman's drumming on the table with his fingers.

"I wish we could all get out of here already. I've had enough of the Regal!"

"Look who's talking! You already have an invitation for an interview, but what can we say?" Teenie stares bitterly at her coffee cup as she keeps stirring it.

"Single girls seem to be having a harder time of it, screw it," Whiskers leans back in his chair.

"But we've been rotting here for over two months," Teenie raises her voice.

"Compared to the residents of room number eight, screw it, you have little to complain of, screw it."

I say goodnight to Nina too, but she doesn't respond. Mathman drags me out of the building with him, telling me not to give her another thought.

"These chicks are like that, they get upset if you screw them, and the same thing if you don't," he explains on the way to our building.

As soon as we enter our room Baldy seeks me out with a plastic shopping bag in hand. His face is easy to read; he's down in the dumps.

"Had supper yet?" he asks.

"Haven't had a thing since breakfast."

"Come, join me," saying that he makes for the table.

"How about beer?"

"I've got it," he glances at the bag.

"How's your pal from number eight?"

"I went to see him in the hospital. He'd had surgery on both of his legs."

We start eating.

140

And sipping beer with every bite.

"Today it was my turn to get lucky. Got my invitation to an interview," a momentary smile flits across his face.

"And you've been waiting all this time to tell me? Hurray for you! Congratulations!"

"It'd taken so long that I cannot work up a feeling of jubilation about it."

"Is that why you're treating me to supper?"

"Partly yes. I didn't feel like eating alone. I haven't been feeling too good lately. Not my old self."

"You have any aches and pains?"

"No, not really. I've been in a lousy mood lately. I mean really depressed."

"In that case I recommend you come with me to the work plaza tomorrow. Work…"

"…cures everything," Baldy relaxes with a smile and upends the bottle to his lips.

* * * *

Next morning finds the two of us in the work plaza. It's cold. Even the tree trunks have goose bumps.

We jump up and down and bump into each other to keep warm.

But no car stops, no takers. It's already nine o'clock when a long black limo pulls up to the curb. The driver, dressed in black uniform and wearing a peaked hat, gets out.

"We need five men," he speaks to Baldy.

"There are only two of us now," I quickly cut in. "What's the job?"

"Interior renovation in the center of Vienna."

"Specifically?"

"Wall and woodwork painting, wallpaper hanging."

"OK, and what's the pay?"

"Market rate, the same as you people usually get. We always hire from here."

"What about it? Let's take it!" I look to Baldy for his assent.

"Okay with me!"

"But bring three more workers."

"We can't today, but I promise for tomorrow," says Baldy

"Well then, hop in," the driver even opens the door for us to the back seat.

It's nice and warm inside. An old pop song is playing on the radio. A pleasant perfume smell rises from the immaculate seats. I have never seen a car like this up close, let alone sit in one.

"And it has A.C. too," says the chauffeur over his shoulder to see how I ogle the dashboard.

"Yes, of course," I agree politely, but then I lean back in the seat to discourage further explanations.

It takes us quite a while to crawl from the outskirts into the heart of the city in the slow traffic. I'm getting bored with the ride when we finally stop in front of an ochre yellow, grand old apartment building on a wide, tree-lined avenue of similar imposing structures

A silent elevator whisks us up to the fifth floor. The door we stop at is answered by a tall, middle-aged man in white overall. The driver politely shows us in.

"How come you only brought two?" The white overall speaks with a hoarse growl.

"Three more will come tomorrow. This fellow promised," the driver points to Baldy and takes off.

"I'm the supervisor of the worksite," the man introduces himself. "Just call me Boss. Six others like you are working here. In two months we must finish the job. Every morning I give every hireling his assignment for the day. Based on the speed and quality of the work I decide who can stay who must go. Payday is every Saturday at three in the afternoon. Which one of you has experience in refinishing woodwork?"

I raise my hand.

"And what can you do?" he turns to Baldy.

"Tiling, wall painting,"

After a tour of the eight-room, three-bathroom, one-kitchen apartment the Boss goes into the specifics of each work assignment.

While working we get acquainted with our fellow workers. They tell us that an international realty company bought the apartment, and after renovating it they will put it in the market again. It's all very interesting, all this background info, but what concerns me is whether they pay as promised. The woodwork specialist assigned to the same job as I am says that so far he's always got paid on time and never shor-tchanged. I'm galvanized by the news, and immediately start calculating the sum I will make working here for two weeks. It's a fortune, a true fortune, I'm delirious.

By eight at night I burn the old paint off of three double-width, four-meter-high, six-casement window units and clean the emerging wood surface. It's ready to be sanded with sandpaper and covered with a prime coat, a primer made of chalk powder.

The Boss examines my work as if he had a magnifying lens in his hand, he looks at it not only straight ahead but at an angle, at every edge and every corner.

"Not quite right here, neither is it over here," his finger keeps jumping from one spot to the next.

"Tomorrow I'll check those spots," I answer respectfully even though I don't see what he's talking about. We both know it's going be sanded tomorrow and that should take care of any little bumps still marring the hundred-year old surface of this beautifully curved Sezessionist window.

Baldy too has been busy, tiling about one-third of the small bathroom. The lines are so straight, the surface so even that I cannot help commenting on the job with a word of praise.

On the other hand, the Boss only hems and haws, shaking his head from side to side.

"I'll send the car to pick you up at seven in the morning. I expect the three others you bring to be at least as skilled as you two are if not better," he dismisses us with the admonition.

It's already late evening when we return to the Regal, to the usual blaring sounds of radios and television sets, to the hollers of a circus, the Babel of never-ending arguments.

* * * *

I wake to the torturing thought that I never managed to talk to my family, and they must be worried about me in the absence of any news. It does no good to keep telling myself 'They must have received my letter by now' and 'What could've happened to me, the package may already be there,' this and other palliative phrases fail to do any good; my stomach gets more and more nervous.

Baldy comes back with three boys I never met before. He waves a hand; it's time to get going.

The limousine is parked by the curb. The double exhaust pipes are pumping out fog-colored, nauseating fumes. Yesterday we hit the tail end of the rush hour, but today we're in the middle of it; no sooner do we crawl out of one traffic jam than hit another one. Our driver though does not meekly follow the herd; he finds alternate routes in side streets to get around the congestion and, in spite of the detours, we arrive in front of the ochre building five minutes to eight. This time we're left to our own devices to find our way to the elevator and the apartment; as soon as we step out of the limo the driver steps on the throttle and pulls away from the curb.

Grump already marks the Boss' face even before we get started.

"I expected you fellows here by seven-thirty," he announces as if nervous about missing a train.

"If it hadn't been for the skillful maneuvers of the driver we'd still be sitting in traffic," Baldy sounds aggrieved and free to talk back as we turn to change into work clothes. But the Boss stops him.

"This morning I'll have to send the regular crew to another urgent job. Starting today you five will be working here alone.

The other crew will come back only three weeks from now, I hope."

He tells us to continue on the job we started yesterday. He assigns the new recruits to other jobs.

We're allowed to quit at eight-thirty at night. By then I finish sanding and priming the stripped surfaces of two gigantic window units. Baldy again excels at his tiling job.

The Boss fires one of the three new recruits.

"Bring someone else, someone who actually has some experience," he raises his voice as he admonishes Baldy on our departure.

I'm utterly exhausted. These two days have been too much for me. But tomorrow is Saturday, payday, and the thought of it gives me an immediate lift.

We have ten minutes before closing time in the food store. We race up and down the aisles to gather the most essential staples.

We eat our late supper without a word in the cacophony of our dormitory room. Baldy clicks open two gold seal bottles of beer. He hands me one of them.

My body is so grateful for the rest that as soon as I hit the sack I fall asleep regardless of the ceiling lamp shining straight into my eyes and the noise assaulting my eardrums.

At dawn, I'm aroused by Baldy shaking my arm. "You have five minutes; I've overslept too this morning."

We run to the gate. The limo is waiting by the curb. Silver clouds of smoke roll out in the back.

"Luckily, already last night I lined up another worker. Introduce yourself," Baldy urges the young man.

Saturday morning, the traffic is much lighter. We are there, ringing the bell by the apartment entrance shortly after seven-thirty. Boss is waiting for us with the same grumpy expression.

"Did you bring the new man?" he yells at Baldy as if he couldn't be bothered to count to five.

I work without stopping till noon. I'm making good progress.

Boss comes by before lunch break to checks out the freshly painted surfaces. He subjects the casements to lengthy scrutiny and then hurries on without a comment.

All the while I'm obsessing with the money I'm making. And the pleasure of achievement. I keep calculating and recalculating the total sum coming to me if I include the following week as well. Except, of course, I'll have to skip Tuesday, the day of the big interview.

Three o'clock comes in no time at all. And then it passes. Boss tells us to keep working, the big chief should be here any minute.

Four o'clock comes and goes, still nothing. We keep working; Why not, if we get paid for it? Every hour counts.

It's already past five when Boss announces we can go home, there'll be no payday today. The big chief called to the other apartment on the floor with the message: his car broke down a hundred kilometers from the city and he's not going to get here today.

Needless to say, the news deflates my spirit.

"Anyone who works tomorrow will get time and a half."

"How long is the workday?" one of the new boys inquires.

"Only till three in the afternoon."

"In that case, I'll come."

At the end we all agree to put in another day's work.

* * * *

Sunday we get back to the Regal around half past four. I feel like taking a nap. But Whiskers stops me; for some reason he's in high spirits and urges me to join him on a visit to the girls.

Teenie greets us with freshly-brewed coffee and immediately starts questioning me about my week, what I've been doing with myself. Looking at Nina sitting next to me I unburden myself with dramatic flourish:

"I've been dreaming about her, and in my dreams she wants me and we sleep together."

146

"Can't you come up with a new line?" turning red, Nina leaps to her feet.

"Take it easy, you two, go easy, screw it. Here's the key, screw it," Whiskers tosses the leather key pouch toward me, "do me a favor, go and get it over with already, screw it!"

Nina rushes out of the room, slamming the door behind her. Blondie playfully slaps Whiskers on the cheek.

"You don't have to be so crude about it. What have you got against that poor girl?"

"What? I'll tell you, I can't stand the way she puts on airs, playing the innocent virgin, screw it, and who knows what kind of life she led back at home, screw it. Here's this fine young man, a regular fellow, hardworking, truthful, and there's no reason why she should not let him have a little pussy. He deserves it, screw it."

"Thanks," I pat Whiskers' shoulder as I get up and start for the door. "But you don't have to be so vehement and direct about it."

"Father Petri was looking for you today. You had an appointment with him at nine-thirty in the chapel," Blondie called out to me on my way out.

"Yeah, I'd forgotten all about it. I've been working all week, including today. It's a nice little job and it pays well," I keep making my apologies as if I were in a confessional.

"He said if you don't show up next Sunday, he'll send out a search team for you. And he means it, too. Don't complain I didn't warn you. Well, see you later. Go get some rest," she dismisses me.

In the park I run into Nina. She's all set on passing me by, but ever so tenderly I get hold of her.

"Please, don't be mad at Whiskers, you know how uncouth, how outspoken he can be. That's what he's like. Same thing when it comes to me, please, don't take offense."

"Just leave me alone," she takes her hand back.

"Have I been harassing you? No. Once I indicated I wanted you. You turned me down. And that was that."

"Every time we meet, you bring up the subject. Why harping on it?"

"Because I still want you."

"It won't work. We're both in a committed relationship. You have a family, and I'm engaged."

"Yes, but now we're both in limbo."

By this time, we're approaching the courtyard. I am about to say goodbye when Nina suddenly puts her arms around me and presses her body against mine.

"Actually, I kind of like you too. If you want, I can give you a hand job," she whispers into my ear.

"I don't really need help with that," I answer in the same soft tone and gently extricate myself from her embrace.

"In that case, have a nice evening."

"You too, Nina," I smile at her and then turn toward the stairs of my building.

I run into Wiseman in the corridor.

"I hear you have a new job. I have not seen much of you in the past few days. You don't take my advice, you're not studying. Someday you'll be sorry."

"The day after tomorrow I'll be going to an interview."

"So soon?"

"I bragged about it to everyone last week."

"Now that you mention it, I seem to recall."

"Heavens! Good thing the subject came up. I need to buy a pair of shoes. It's completely escaped my memory."

"The stores will be open tomorrow."

"Yeah, but I leave for work at dawn and don't get back until very late."

"Run out in lunch break. And how about language lessons?" he raises a finger in the air between us.

"I'll work this coming week, but I promise to start studying if the interview goes well. And what's on your program?"

"There's a missionary group here from the States. They give two one-hour classes every day, and conversation practice in the evening. Plus, Bible study sessions. I spend the rest of my free time reading and studying."

"I'll definitely take your advice when I get around to it. You bet I'll be busy as a bee."

In our dorm room there's another big ruckus waiting for us. Impossible to tell what started it. Just happens. I'm badly in need of rest. I have a difficult week ahead of me. Sleep catches me totally unawares; I just blissfully conk out.

* * * *

By the time Baldy and I step out the Regal gate our three fellow workers are already waiting for us. But there's no sign of the limousine yet, and it's already five minutes past seven.

"So far he's always been ahead of time, waiting for us." As usual, I expect the worst. Whatever it is.

"Don't get yourself into a tizzy, he'll be here soon enough," Baldy's not worried.

At seven-fifteen the limo shows up at the intersection.

I breathe a sigh of relief.

"I don't understand why you're always stressed out," Baldy snarls at me as he shows me into the vehicle.

"Sorry, fellows," says the chauffeur. "I didn't get to bed until late last night and overslept this morning."

"It's all right with us, but how about Boss? What's he going to say about us being late?" I worry again.

"Let him say what he wants, that's his job," the driver shrugs it off.

It's eight-twenty when we pull up in front of the big apartment house. As soon as we get out the car is gone.

Boss greets us with an expression that's beyond grouchy; it's somber.

"Why so late?" he growls at us.

Why ask us? Remaining respectful, we refrain from stating the obvious; he knows that we know that he knows we're not responsible for our transport. But he's Boss.

"To make up for the late start we'll have to cut the lunch break by a half an hour," he renders his verdict and starts handing out assignments for the day.

All morning I'm consumed by the problem of buying a pair of shoes for the interview. Will I have enough time for it? In my more lucid moments, I can put aside this picayune concern. What's the big deal? In worst case scenario I can wear the one and only pair of shoes I possess. Who cares if it doesn't match my new suit?

At lunchtime Boss informs us we will not be getting our overdue pay for last week, because the big chief had to take a trip somewhere. But not to worry, we only worked a few days last week, and the payment will be added to this week's wages on Saturday.

We acknowledge the news with heads bent, looking at the floor yet to be refinished. None of us has a question.

I do speak up, but only say I have to run out for a half an hour to go shopping.

"If you're not back in time I'll take it out of your pay," Boss grants permission pointing at the door to hurry me up.

Twenty minutes later and out of breath I stumble back into the apartment.

Success!

As soon as I was out in the street I asked the first passerby about the nearest shoe store. He gave me directions; the place was only two blocks away, not too far to walk.

I show Baldy my purchase.

He nods without comment.

I'm happy with it. A pair of black shoes, wide at the tip, not pointed. They will go well with my gray suit.

* * * *

Eight o'clock, quitting time.

We've made good progress. At this rate I should finish all the windows by Saturday night, leaving only the doors to be done. Baldy finished tiling the second bathroom. He should get the walls of the whole kitchen refinished by the end of the week. I make my excuses to Boss concerning the next day; I will not be able to make it to work on account of an interview I'll have to attend.

"What kind of an interview?" he asks suspiciously.

"At the Canadian Embassy. Concerning my immigration application."

"Yeah," he snarls back. "But you'd better show up Wednesday!"

"At seven in the morning, as usual, I'll be waiting for transport," I walk out the door feeling very good with myself.

Baldy notices the change in me, too; wonders what has cheered me up so suddenly. But I see no point in going into details. He's got his own problems.

We find our dorm room in the middle of celebration. And for good reason: today four immigration applications were granted. Two to the States, one to Canada and one to Australia. Four residents of the room will be flying the coop next week. Instead of angry voices, laughter sets the tone of the Babel tonight, fueled by copious flow of beer. It's a welcome change, everyone's in high spirits.

I try on my new second-hand suit with the newly acquired pair of shoes.

Mathman takes notice.

Even makes a complimentary remark.

I model my gala outfit to Baldy.

"You're all dressed up smartly like Joe Hillbilly for his wedding. Are you quite sure you washed the dung off your feet?" Baldy too is infected by the holiday mood.

Thinking about sleeping late tomorrow keeps me from falling asleep. I feel like an army commander on the eve of a crucial battle. I feel crushed by the weight, the importance of the next day; its outcome will change the course of my life. At the same time the nagging question remains: What if I don't get accepted by Canada? What's going to happen to me?

151

There's still Australia, another possibility, I hasten to assure myself. Something will have to happen.

One thing is certain: I've got to get away from here. I keep saying and rephrasing this sentence in my head until finally I fall asleep.

* * * *

I'm standing in the door of a streetcar, about to descend, when I get assaulted by a sudden gust of wind. For a split second my body feels like a boat without an anchor. Another breath and I regain my balance, ready to step down to the sidewalk. My light raincoat snaps open on my chest. It's bone-chilling weather.

In hardly any time at all I find the address indicated in the invitation.

It's only ten-thirty, I could pass the time by taking a walk. Buffeted by the wind though, I soon change my mind and head back to the main entrance of the embassy building.

Inside I'm confronted by two armed guards. I show them the letter from the embassy. They direct me to a bullet-proof glass cage, a doorman's box.

I slip the letter into the cage, and the man inside examines it. He sends me to a room one floor up, the elevator is to the right.

The room turns out to be a comfortable though Spartan waiting room with straight-back chairs against the wall. Some of them are occupied by a young couple with children and a single man about my age.

I make my way to the receptionist's counter.

I hand over the embossed envelope.

A middle-aged lady takes it and scrutinizes it before looking up my name on a list in front of her.

"Do you have a Regal card?" she asks With a smile.

I hand it over.

She draws a circle around the numeral 13 by my name on the list.

"Take a seat and wait until you're called."

Dozens of thoughts rush to my mind. I cannot sort them out, they're much too malleable, almost liquid. Their confluence is impossible to stop. My heart is beating in my throat, like before an exam in school.

Sitting on a chair I follow with my eyes the two children at play on the carpet.

Time doesn't stand still in the waiting room. More and more people enter. The young man is called in and then the family of four is swallowed up by another door.

And yet minutes pass by as if weighed down by lead. They barely budge.

Why aren't they calling me in? I feel the question stab me in the chest.

A lady who came after me gets to her feet and walks toward the door of the inner office. Three others follow in her footsteps at irregular intervals.

Hearing my name called I leap to my feet, but then I stop, unsure whether I really heard it or just imagined it.

"Go ahead, go inside," two people from the two sides of the door speak to me with encouragement.

I find myself in a spacious office. Behind the heavy desk a man in a brown tweed jacket is riffling through a bunch of papers. Noticing me, he points to a chair nearby. We're not alone; in the corner, with her back to me, a white-haired lady is rummaging in a bookcase.

On hearing me pull the chair closer to the desk she leaves the corner and joins me in another chair.

"I'm your interpreter," she extends a hand with a smile. "This gentleman is the consul. I will be translating his questions, and, of course, your answers. I ask you to keep to the point and be concise. Are you ready?"

"Yes, absolutely," I say with some effort; my mouth has just dried up.

"Take a sip," she pushes a glass of water closer to me.

The consul leans back in his swivel chair and asks me to tell him the story of my escape across the border.

153

My narrative is halting at the beginning, but it doesn't take me long to warm up to the subject of my headlong run.

"What was the name of the old man, the hired guide?"

"I don't know. We met at someone else's house and he got very angry when I asked him what to call him."

They both have a wide grin on hearing this detail.

"How do you spend your days at the Regal?"

"I work whenever I get a chance. I need the money; I have to support my family by sending them packages.

"Where do you work? Refugees do not get work permit, they're not allowed to take jobs."

"That's true, but if we stand in front of the Regal we get hired for the day or even longer."

"I see you have a new suit."

"Yes, my work at the coffee plant paid for it. And the shoes, too. But only the footwear is new, the suit is from a second-hand store."

"Were you employed at the coffee plant?" The consul sounds surprised.

"Yes. Well, not really, they had me working without any papers filled out. And only for one week. No one works there longer than a week. That's the rule."

The grins return.

"Suppose you immigrate to Canada; would you like to have your family follow you?"

"I wouldn't abandon them for the world."

"You will have to prove you can support them before you can apply for their immigration."

"First thing I'll learn the language and I'll work. I'm a jack of all trades, I expect no problem getting a job."

"But suppose you have to go north, suppose there's no other work except in the lumber industry, would you be willing to become a lumberjack?"

"Sure. Why not? It wouldn't have to be a lifetime commitment... I'm sure I wouldn't have to spend the rest of my life chopping wood."

The interpreter lady laughs as she translates.

The consul echoes her.

But then it's back to business. More questions. What was I doing for a living back home, where did I go to school, was I ever a member of the Party, who were my friends, what were my parents' professions? Plus a thousand other things. My head is spinning when finally the interview comes to an end.

"Thank you," the consul relaxes by holding a pencil between two fingertips. "We're finished here, but some of my colleagues may have further questions, so we ask you to stay around a little longer in the waiting room. Be patient, you'll be called."

On my way out I wonder if said goodbye or thank you, but it's too late, I'm already in the door, I might stumble if I turn back.

Sitting again in the waiting room.

My patience is running out.

I listen hard whenever a name is called lest I miss hearing mine.

I'm pretty sure my name has not been called yet.

People are called one by one and directed to another side door.

Silence returns.

Beyond a door a copying machine is clanking out its product; its noise is tempered by the machinegun fire of heavy office typewriters.

Footfalls echo from the parquet floor to the high stucco ceiling.

Doors slam shut.

Silence sets in again for a while.

Vanishing worlds pass before my eyes.

A rainbow appears to me, the feathers of exotic birds in the arcades of infinity.

My fatigue lifts, my body feels weightless, my thoughts come and go like lazy summer breezes.

I awake on hearing my name called for the third time.

I stagger to the counter, still not quite sure if I heard it right.

"Me?" I point a finger at my chest.

The lady nods.

"Were you asleep?" she gives me a funny look.

"Could be. I've been working hard lately and not getting enough sleep. Please excuse my weakness…"

"I'll ask you to sign these papers by the X mark, here, and here, and there. Thank you. Here's you Regal card back. On this sheet there's a complete list of things for you to do. And here's an order for a medical exam and another for an X-ray. You can get them done at the Regal. They will know how to handle these in the infirmary. Thank you and congratulations on the success of your interview!" She hands over a pack of papers through the narrow window. On second thought, she whips out a manila envelope to hold all the documents.

What started out as a routine, tedious bureaucratic procedure suddenly became a personal victory. The pride of achievement fills me with unexpected feeling of warmth. I hold the papers with great pride as if I had a winning lottery ticket in my hand. Indeed, it may turn out to be that, too, but for now the freedom it promises is enough for me to celebrate.

I couldn't care less about the freezing temperature, the cloudy sky when I step out to the street, delirious with triumph. "Asylum granted, I'm in, accepted! You hear that God? I've been accepted!" I feel like shouting, but the next moment I look around to see if there's anyone nearby to hear me, in case I let it slip out.

The street is empty, as if swept clean by the wind.

The whole city looks different; in the boulevard the passersby look friendly now as if they knew of my new status.

And I don't try to hide it either.

Even the finicky gusts of wind fail to wither the smile on my face.

The wrinkles of the weather smooth out. The buildings put on a happy façade, the trees keep pace with me. The passengers in the cars sliding by me seem to look at me with admiration.

The jubilation inside me knows no bounds.

The traffic noise modulates into a soothing ostinato, and the large, colorful flag on top of a high cupola flaps as if to greet me, congratulating me.

Existence is a fully packed wagon, filled with unexpected things of all kinds.

Now it has opened a gift box for me, too.

I don't keep an eye on the time, I couldn't care less; for the first time here I look at the city like an aimless tourist taking in the sights, and I find everything just magnificent! Anxiety is so far from me now as if it had never resided in me, torturing me without end. But the end is nigh!

A new beginning is budding into fresh flowers, producing new longings, new fears.

But who cares about the distant future?

Let it come, whatever it brings!

Shop windows gleam back at me, wherever I look.

All is glitter and light.

A restaurant catches my attention on the corner.

Out front, it has a life-size chef figure, cut out of plywood, holding a board with the day's menu scrawled on it with crayon: seared goose liver, chicken breast, oven-roasted suckling pig, beef tenderloin with pineapple. My mouth is salivating. I can't resist the temptation, step inside.

After the pleasant meal I purchase a greeting card at a newsstand. I want to pour out my heart on it, but it can hold no more than this short message: "My dearly beloved, I send you good tidings! Canada has accepted me, I just finished the interview. A few days ago I tried to call you. I waited for hours to hear your voices but without success. Kisses and hugs, your loving Dad."

It's dark already when I get back to the Regal.

Mathman is asleep, flat on his back, with his hands clasped on his stomach. He's awakened when I start climbing to my bunk.

"Tell me, what happened? Success?" he asks as soon as he opens his eyes.

"They accepted me," I answer, trying to sound indifferent.

157

"No joking?"

"Here it is, in black and white," I pull the envelope from my pocket. "All I need is a physical and a valid passport and I'll be on my way. Flying."

"Good Heavens! You're on track!" he shouts at me. "I'd give my soul for that!"

But he's not done with me yet. He wants me to give him every detail of the interview, every question I was asked. In particular, he wants to know if they gave me a hard time trying prove I was an economic refugee. He gets so emotionally involved with questioning me that I can't help it, I have to burst out laughing.

"You laughing at me? Am I so ridiculous?" he sounds offended.

"No, not at all," I try to placate him. "But the way you are questioning me sounds more like an interrogation, as if you were trying to get some vital information out of me."

"You've got over the big stumbling block, you're all set. But not me! I still have the big interview ahead of me."

"Don't worry about it. As I understand it, you're in a privileged position. You have not only your bride waiting for you but a job, a house all picked out, a family coming along in the future, but what have I got waiting for me? Nothing. Nothing but loneliness and the struggle to make a living. And who knows when I'll get to see my family."

Mathman calms down, nodding in assent. He lies back in his bunk and closes his eyes.

"There are a lot of unknown factors in my future, too. It may look like to you that everything is going great for me, but things are never that simple," he says softly, almost like a confession, and clasps his hands on his stomach again.

Waiting for Baldy I stretch out on the bunk, still in my street clothes and fall asleep. I wake up at midnight to find the room dark already, an unusual situation. Only the yellowish lights of the streetlamps make it possible for me to orient myself. I quickly undress and in minutes I'm back to sleep.

"Wakeup time! I want the Canadians to move a little faster," Baldys's voice is trumpeting by my bed .

"Good morning, last night I fell asleep waiting for you to show up."

"I didn't get home until real late. That old grouch, Boss, had me remove three rows of tiles from the kitchen wall. He claimed they were crooked. Uneven."

"So?"

"So what? I smashed them and scraped them off. What else could I do? I worked until ten-thirty. And that guy was just standing there with me all the time, until I redid the whole thing."

"I don't want to think about what to expect when I get in to work today. By the way, I'll be late today, I'll have to get the physical exam done this morning."

"Okay, I'll tell Boss when we get in. But don't dawdle too late. Yesterday he wanted to fire one fellow who was ten minutes late getting back from lunch break."

I linger in bed almost till nine. I'm not used to it. Although impatience is trying hard to roust me out of bed, I listen to the calm voice of reason that assures me: "Why bother? The infirmary doesn't open till nine-thirty."

Gaining the courtyard, I turn right, but after a few steps I find course correction is in order back to the left; it occurs to me I owe all this to Madam Olga and I should let her know that. She should get the good news directly from me rather than through an impersonal report a few days later.

The waiting room is filled with new faces, but I happen to know the boy sitting by the door and ask him if there's anyone in with the administrator. He says no, there's no one in.

I knock on the door and start opening it.

"Come in, my lad," Madam Olga welcomes me with a smile. "How did it go yesterday? Your interview?"

"Would you believe it? They accepted me!" By now I've said it so many times that the momentum is gone from the phrase and so is the joy that animated it yesterday as if the spirit had lost its initial arousal.

"I knew it, I felt it in my bones, you were poised for success. In the past few months the Canadians have speeded up their immigration process. You'll be flying sometime in the first part of December."

"You mean in a couple of weeks?"

"Yes. Why? Are things moving too fast for you? Haven't you put in enough time at the Regal?"

"Much too much! But I can hardly believe the end is near. And what are we going to do about the Australian interview?"

"That's why I recommended Canada. The Aussies seem to take forever with their bureaucratic ways."

"Yes, but I had my heart set on it…"

"How many times do I have to tell you," Madam Olga interrupts my wistful words, "the world doesn't run according to our dreams. You should thank God you can get out of here because you have a place to go."

"I have a job this week, but next week, I promise, I'll be here decorating your office," I exit on this line.

I don't have long to wait in the medical office. My turn comes, they take blood, a doctor gives me a perfunctory exam. Goes through the usual ritual with the stethoscope on my chest, front and back. Asks if I have any medical problems. Next it's the chest x-ray. I'm made to stand before the machine. Click. The doctor gets hold of my hands and spins me around slowly.

"There are two spots in the right lobe. They look like vestiges of childhood infections. Do you recall any problems growing up?" he asks while turning me to see my right side again.

"I used to have very painful middle-ear infections, but I don't recall anything else."

"That's all right, we'll take a picture."

I'm pressed against the tablet holding the film.

"Don't move! Hold your breath!"

Click.

160

"All done, you can step aside."

While putting on my shirt again in the dim light of the examination room I can't help observing that the doctor is slowly tilting his head from side to side, lost in thought.

"Any problems?" I almost choke on my voice.

"I see something, but I'm not sure what. I'll have to send this x-ray to the central office and let them check it out. If they decide they need additional pictures they'll let you know."

I sense concern and commiseration in his tone.

"Nothing to worry about. Nowadays there's treatment for everything, sometimes even complete cure." He adds on a brighter note.

I stumble out to the quadrangle in a state of upheaval. Spots on my lung, I keep repeating the words to myself.

I go over my childhood memories. My colds were always accompanied by awful earaches, and now I can picture those feverish days and nights, all the pills I had to take with or without a meal, the painful injections. And the frequent x-rays. A doctor's lean face, his pencil moustache and his black-framed glasses equipped with a jeweler's magnifier emerge from the murky past. I wish I could ask my mother about all these things, I'm sure she'd set my mind at ease.

Lunch break is about to come to a close when I arrive at my work place. Boss looks at me with baleful eyes.

"It sure took you some time, this doctor's visit."

"They don't open until nine-thirty. I came here as soon as I could get away," I make no effort to hide my discontent.

I start working without further delay.

It's hard for me to make any headway, impossible to concentrate on the job. My thoughts keep wandering off. I'm possessed by forebodings.

"Tell me, what happened?" Baldy turns to me as we step out of the elevator in the evening.

"It's not quite clear what, but there's something wrong with my lungs."

"In what way?"

"They see spots, sclerosis, as the doctor explained."

161

"Pay no heed to him, these doctors always find something wrong just so they can make you worry," Baldy tries to brush it off, but I seem to detect the same tone of commiseration that the doctor had for me.

I don't get much rest the following night. Hardly any sleep at all. By dawn the sheet under me and the blanket over me are inextricably entwined. In the short intervals asleep I have dreams in Technicolor flash through my mind but then vanish as soon as I try to conjure them again. I can only recall the recurring images of the high cliff and the huge black birds roosting on it.

Baldy's all set to go, impatient for me to get ready.

"I don't understand what's happening to me. I feel as if a thousand dwarves had been battering me with their mini size clubs," I explain as we cut across the Regal court.

Boss greets us with the same morose look as always. The same scene greets us all week, even Saturday morning when we enter the apartment with spirits flying high. Payday!

The enjoyment I usually find in work returns. We're making good progress. Three of our coworkers have hung every room with tapestry, leaving only finishing touches for today. Baldy too is done with the tiling job. He needs to even out the grout and then wash off the tiled surfaces.

As far as my job is concerned, I'm all done with the windows and ready to start on the doors, but the completion would require another week.

At lunchtime I can hardly swallow any food, so excited I am. I keep calculating and re-calculating the wages I earned with the number of hours and days worked. In my estimate I should get enough money to last me till my departure for Canada without having to take on another job. Maybe now I'll be able to relax and take language lessons.

It's past three in the afternoon. Boss takes a tour of the apartment informing us that the big chief is on his way with the wages owed to us.

But it's already past four when the doorbell rings.

Boss is nearest and it's he who strolls over to answer it.

An armed policeman enters the foyer. He's followed by three more. One of them locks the door and takes the key.

Two of them stand guard in the living room while a third herds us together.

"Come on, let me see your identity papers!" demands a mustachioed cop, the oldest one among them, probably a sergeant.

All five of us hand over our Regal cards.

Seeing the cards the lead cop produces a deprecating grin.

"You people are no doubt aware of the fact that you're breaking the law. This card does not entitle you to a work permit. So what are you doing here?"

None of us has an answer.

"And you sir? May I see your papers?" he turns to Boss who seems to oblige with conspicuous readiness. He pulls his ID card from a fat leather wallet and hands it over as if he were showing a picture of his newborn son. Far from like a thief caught in the act, he behaves like a congenial, long-term acquaintance.

"There you go," he hands over his bona fides.

The sergeant mumbles something and then hands it back. He takes a notebook from an inside pocket and copies our names from the Regal cards before giving them back to us.

"First thing Monday morning I'll report you gentlemen to the Regal command, citing you for illegal labor practices. And now I order you all to get your stuff and clear out of here. I don't ever want to see you people here again. Understand?"

Fright, despair, fury, thoughts of revenge swirl inside me. I look at myself and my fellow slaves with contempt, the way we hurry to obey, hopping to the command, collecting our wretched bags, jackets and shopping bags. Like defeated rabble on the rout we file out the apartment door.

At the end of the block we stop to recoup.

163

"Let's watch for the cops. As soon as they're gone we go back for our pay. After all, we've worked for every penny," one of the wallpaper-hangers suggests.

In a short while three cops emerge from the building. They stop to look up and down the street.

We hide around the corner, peering out with one eye.

They walk about fifty meters to a squad car parked by the curb.

They get in, make a U-turn and take off in the opposite direction.

"All clear, let's go upstairs!" the wallpaper man speaks up again.

"Didn't you see? Only three cops left, the fourth is still upstairs." Baldy stops him. "We'd better wait a few more minutes."

One minute follows another and after a half an hour we're still watching the situation from our hiding place around the corner.

We take turns keeping n eye on the entrance, but none of us detects anyone coming or going from the building.

"Is it possible the building may have a back entrance?" I pose the question.

Without answering Baldy takes off at a trot for the next cross street.

He returns in ten minutes, his eyes red with unsuppressed anger.

"It's got not one but two back entrances. I went up to the fifth floor, I rang the bell, not once but several times and for a long time, but no answer," Baldy reports, still out of breath.

"I can't believe it. We worked ten days for nothing," one of the tapestry boys sighs. "all because it was cheaper for Boss to pay off the cops than give us our slave wages..."

We can't seem to get over it. How could anyone just take his losses and move on? We hang out on the same spot, on the corner. Everyone has something to bring to the debate, explanations, small cautionary signs we ignored, Boss'

164

gestures, the postponed payday last Saturday, and a number of other things we blame on one another.

Only too soon, the verbal post mortem of our misadventure turns into a loud, almost physical brawl.

We've exhausted all accusations, imprecations and curse words by the time we get back into our dorm room.

Baldy is so upset with me that he's stopped talking. If I say anything, he demonstratively turns his head in the other direction. At one point he even blames the whole thing on my workaholic and foolish nature; without that he would not have gone out to the work plaza.

Later I ask him to join me for supper, but he refuses to sit at the same table with me.

Munching my meager meal alone I start wondering if should try my luck again on the work plaza. My savings have gone way down lately.

And then, inevitably, my thoughts turn to my folks back home. I wish I could hear from them. The lung X-ray another unexpected obstacle, another cause for worry. It also occurs to me tomorrow is Sunday, and I promised Father Petri to attend his mass.

I'd better take this Sunday off, I decide while brushing my teeth. I need to regain my mental and emotional equilibrium. Let my calvary resume its course Monday morning.

I sleep until eight and wake up more tired than I was getting into bed.

From my perch I can see Baldy lying motionless, his blanket half off.

The bunk below me is empty. Mathman obviously spent Saturday night outside somewhere. Most likely he took Teenie to a classier joint; as spacious as that jalopy is, it's not an ideal place for a night of romantic, sensuous love. That last word though gives me pause. I can't help but linger over it.

I walk into the chapel at nine-fifteen, ahead of the appointed time. It's larger than one would expect to find in a facility like this. It has regular church pews, divided by an aisle in the middle, but the altar is a simple table with a silk-like cover over it. On the back wall there's a massive crucifix that sets the tone of the place.

The double door slams shut behind me with a bigger bang than appropriate in a place of worship, and it results in the appearance of Father Petri from a hidden opening in a corner of the back wall like a shadow coming alive.

"Laudatur..."

"In aeternam, amen. Come in, this way," he beckons to me.

"The last time something came up, and it didn't work out for me..."

"Come, let's sit down and have a chat," he turns toward the opening that he emerged from.

I obey the commandment.

We enter a simply furnished open space, more like an alcove that also serves as sacristy. The priest takes one chair and offers me the other.

"Since the last time we met I've taken it upon myself to find out more about you. Madam Olga describes you as a diligent and disciplined young man with a goal in life," he gives me a look that's not casual but meant to bore deep into the other's mind and search it for all the essentials in the short time available to such a busy servant of God.

"That sounds good, but unfortunately, it's far from a complete picture, Father."

"Yes, I understand, the everyday temptations fill in the gaps. But that's no news, it's been the human condition ever since the world began. Man piles sin upon sin counting on washing them away with the blood Christ spilt for us. But as Horace said in a letter: *'It's your heart you have to change and not the vault of the sky above you.'* In other words, you take your sins with you wherever you go. Life is immortal and it in God's hands," he speaks to me with his eyes constantly trying to meet mine as a way of inducing me to fall in with his line of reasoning.

"When was the last time you went to confession?"

"When I was still in my childhood, Father."

166

"Don't you dare partake in the Holy Communion today!"

"No, certainly not, Father."

He's enraged; the way he looks at me could leave me seriously injured.

He certainly makes me feel I'm a habitual sinner who wallows in mortal sins, not just plain venial ones. I can hardly wait to get this interview over with.

We part as polite but deliberate strangers.

During the mass our eyes often meet, but every time he's the one to shift his gaze.

Blondie is in the same pew, just an arm's length from me. She sings the psalms and repeats the prayers with sincere piety. During homily she looks at me with her eyebrows raised in a question mark. I signal to her to wait until it's over.

I find the ceremony wearisome to the point being unbearably endless. I'm eager to pour out my soul to Blondie and ask her why she introduced me to this especially dour servant of God. He seems to believe the whole world is a big detention camp, a den of iniquities. I certainly didn't need this extra burden on my shoulders.

At the end of the mass I walk out to the corridor and stop there waiting for Blondie. But there's no sign of her. Every time the door opens, I take a quick look but I can't see her anywhere. Finally, there she is, stepping across the threshold by the side of Father Petri.

"*'The seer is in rage: can he ever tear that great god out of his heart!'* isn't that right, my lad?"

"*'I was not born for a single little dale, my homeland is the whole world.'*" I am quick to answer his quote with one of mine.

"Not so fast, my young friend, God must be welcome everywhere! Keep that in mind. If you don't, you'll lose that world where you feel so comfortable with yourself."

"He's a good boy, Father," Blondie tries heroically to save the situation.

"Then take good care of him, especially his sinful soul," the priest puts on a thin smile and rushes off.

When the dark cassock is far enough from us, Blondie tears into me.

"What happened? Did you two have a scrap?"

"No, not at all, it's just that I was open with him. I simply told him what was on my mind," I brush off her concerns.

"That was a serious mistake. The old man is very rigid, unwilling to compromise, very obstinate in a debate. And you're determined to take him on!"

"Are you trying to pick a fight with me?"

"Who's fighting? Calm down! You're talking to a friend, not an enemy. Lucky thing he heard nothing but good about you in the registration office. Don't get all worked up about it needlessly, the old man will simmer down. But let me tell you, he's got very good memory. And now come over and have coffee with us. Go get hold of Whiskers, tell him I'm waiting for him."

How did I screw this up? I'm upset with myself and with always feeling despondent.

I climb the stairs in a hurry as if to leave my troubles behind. To my surprise I run into Wiseman in the company of the opera singer and the young lady with a daughter.

"Let me introduce my friend!"

"We already know each other," says the artiste. "We met in the medical office."

"Is that so?" Wiseman nods as if he had arranged the meeting and then turns to me. "Imagine that! In two weeks all three of them will be flying to the States!"

"Good to hear some good news for a change," I smile at him the sincerely, but something piques my curiosity. I ask Wiseman to step aside for a second.

When we're out of earshot of the ladies, I ask him in a whisper:

"Are both of them your lovers?"

"No, no, only one of them. The younger one."

"Ah-ah. You never mentioned it."

"Why should I have? Live and let live. The gal says she's willing to divorce her husband and marry me when we get out there."

"Why should she marry a madman like you?"

"Because she loves me. Understand what I mean? She loves me!"

We rejoin the ladies. I wish them the best of luck in the New World and say goodbye to them.

I hurry on to get hold of Whiskers as instructed by Blondie. However, in spite of all my nudging he's not willing to get out of bed because... he's not.

When I step out to the court alone, I realize how overcast and unfriendly the sky is. But I find the cool breeze rather bracing. I feels good. I unzip my jacket to let my overheated body cool off.

I stay out in the park, just wandering around for quite a while.

* * * *

"How would this potted flower look over here, on this plate?" I turn to Madam Olga. "And I think the job is done. What do you think?"

"Incredible how much you could achieve on a minimal budget!"

"One part imagination, one part improvisation and one part patience," I explain while surveying the results of my labor for a final evaluation.

The lady apparently notices the bitterness tugging at my polite smile. She suddenly gets back to business.

"It's much too early to make a tragedy out of the lung X-ray. Patience, my lad, and all your problems will vanish eventually. I spoke to the doctor yesterday. He says the Canadians are overly cautious about any disease that has to do with the lungs. In his opinion we should wait until the central public health office renders its judgment and then we take our cue from that."

I take a nap in the afternoon and sleep until eight in the evening. No question about it, I'm beset by problems, but I cannot let them get me down, I must keep my head above water.

Perhaps my biggest problem is my despondency, and that's what I have to fight. And perhaps the only thing that's within my power to fight.

Tomorrow a new day will start, and I'll have to conquer it.

* * * *

I get up a few minutes past seven. No lingering, no lounging this morning. I hurry to the washroom, dress quietly and quickly, before Baldy wakes up and starts taunting me with his irritating remarks.

I'm greeted by more temperate weather outside. The wind is milder and not nearly as cold on the walkway to the gate.

There are four men looking for work this morning in the plaza. I join the line along the curb, but just as I start toying with a small gravel stone with the nose of my show a car comes to a stop by me.

"How about splitting wood," the elderly gentleman inside addresses me through the window.

"Is there a lot?"

"Two truckloads."

"Several days' work."

"Yes."

"What's the pay?"

"Three hundred a day."

"That's very low."

"You don't want the job?"

"Yes, I do."

"Well, then it's agreed. Get in."

We stop in front of a two-story single-family home. We leave the car by the curb. The property is fenced off by a wrought iron grill. The gate opens with a squeak that reminds me of old math teacher by the blackboard underlining the equation for the area of circle.

He leads me directly to the cellar. Tree trunks sawed to firewood length fill the place to the ceiling.

"This job may take a week," I look the employer in the eye.

"It'll take what it will, but I want you to do a good job."

"Of course, sir."

I keep working all morning, putting all my energy into it, without letting up. It feels good to use my muscles gain, the exercise speeds up the blood circulation. In the meantime, my thoughts keep hopping around. I don't bother to hold on to any one of them in particular; as soon as one pops up, I let it run off. It's hard to tell whether I am fleeing them or they're roar off on their own.

In the second hour I'm bathing in a bubble bath of contentment. I figure the job will take about six days. That should make up for last week's loss, or most of it.

"God lives and he's with me!" I want to cry out and bring down the ax with added force.

At noon the old gent comes down to check on my progress. A stack of logs, ready for the fire place is already growing along one wall. Seeing that he nods with a smile and he's about to say something, but then turning to the unfinished pile he looks somber again.

"Come up for lunch," he finally says.

The kitchen is perhaps is not as spacious as it is made to seem by the sleek blond-wood furniture and the faux marble tiles on the walls. In addition, the color scheme creates a sense of harmony.

I find myself confronted by a tall and lean lady wearing wire-rimmed glasses. Her scrutinizing gaze puts me so much ill at ease that I almost forget to deliver a polite greeting.

'Welcome, young man," she responds and points to a seat across the table from her husband.

The meal is the best I've had in a long time; the vegetable soup, generously sprinkled with fresh parsley, is very flavorful, and so is the pork roast that follows. It comes with oven-baked

171

potatoes and sautéd red cabbage. For dessert she serves walnut torte and coffee with whipped cream on top. To wash down the roast the master of the house pours red wine. The meal makes me feel so mellow that I lose all my appetite for work; I'm ready for a little nap.

"Now you should be ready to burn up all the calories you've put away," the old man says with a teasing wink.

"Yes, I have my strength restored, all I need is momentum to get going again."

"Would an espresso help?" the lady offers.

"Yes, please."

I profusely thank her for the meal and go back to the cellar. The first whacks with the ax require extra effort, but soon I get back into the rhythm of the work.

Soon I am haunted by self-lacerating, soul-torturing thoughts. I'm back home again, with my family where I belong.

*

"Don't take the kids to the park today; they'll catch a cold. The wind is fierce and cold. I don't understand why you must always be on the go. Please, I beg you to simmer down. Tomorrow afternoon I'll get out of work sooner and take them for a walk. "

"But listen, the little ones need fresh air. In the park they can play with the others, run around, burn up some excess energy out in the open."

"And are you going to take care of them when they get sick?"

"Yes, absolutely! In the past three and a half years every time they developed a fever it's been my job to look after them."

"That's only because I'm so snowed under with work. You don't seem to care what I have to go through from one class after another so that I can earn our living."

"Are you saying I lie idle all day?"

"No, I didn't mean to say that."

172

"But that's exactly what you said: 'our living'. As if you were the only one in the family struggling to make a living for us all."

"In that case, I'm sorry, okay? I picked the wrong word."

"Exactly!"

"Please, calm down! Let's stop fighting. I'm exhausted and not in the mood for it. Or anything else. Maybe I need a change of scenery, something entirely different, like an open meadow or mountains. You remember when you were courting me we hiked up into the mountainside forest and you made love to me."

"How could I forget? Especially since you stated at that time that I was the first who… in the forest…"

"And you refused to believe it."

"I'm forever the doubting Thomas. No, not really. I'm talking nonsense. Perhaps because I was jealous of the first man you gave yourself to."

"A supposition or a statement…"

"Pretty sure. I was not the first man in your life."

"I never claimed that. I even accounted for every relationship I'd had."

"Almost everyone."

"I could've missed one or two, but I don't remember now."

"You don't?"

"I don't! Because they meant nothing to me. They were faceless figures."

"So there were a number of them?"

"You take every word I say and twist it to suit your imagination. Re-interpret everything I relate to you beyond recognition."

"You know what? In spite of everything I love you beyond reason. Come here, let's hug."

"I love you too, but I wish you'd stop arguing with me all the time."

"That's my wish, too."

"Granted. I promise."

* * * *

At six in the evening I have to quit; the old man comes
down, he's ready to take me back home. Behind me, against
the wall, there are two rows of split logs rising.

He runs a hand over the ends of the logs, perhaps to see if
they're packed tightly enough, the way it looks to me.

In the entrance foyer the lady of the house is waiting for me
with a plastic shopping bag,

"A little leftover roast for supper," she hands over the bag
with a tender tilt of her head. "See you tomorrow morning."

Her concern touches me.

I bow when I say goodbye.

"Walter," she addresses the husband on our way out, "don't
go wandering off, come straight home!"

"My boy, don't ever get married. Wives are all like that,"
says the old man laughing and locks the gate behind us.

"Too late. I made that mistake years ago. I already have two
little boys," I mumble as if talking to myself.

"You look too young for that, to be the head of a family.
God bless them and God bless you. Unfortunately, Helga
miscarried every time. So it's only the two of us. My brother
though has two sons and a daughter. They are our godchildren.
All three of them are married, with five little ones among them.
They're our family. Well, we've arrived. What time can I pick
you up in the morning."

"Would seven-thirty be all right?"

"Perfect. That'll give me until seven to lounge around,"
Walter holds out a hand.

The noise level is unusually low in the dorm room tonight.
Only the radio is on in the far corner by the window. I hurry
directly to Baldy's bed.

"Hi, how are you? I brought home some roast pork," I hale
my friend.

"Where have you been? I've been looking for you all day,"
he growls at me.

174

"I give you one guess."

"You went out to the Work Plaza."

"And I got a job. For the whole week."

"Watch out! Don't let them make a sucker of you again!"

"An elderly couple, retired. Very nice people. At noon they invited me to sit down to lunch with them. Even packed up stuff for supper."

"And what's the job?"

"Splitting firewood. Logs sawed off but not split yet, a whole cellar full of them, waiting to be split for the fireplace."

"How much do you get?"

"Three hundred a day."

"Not bad."

While he gets the supper ready, I run upstairs for two bottles with golden collar. The bootlegger gives me a funny look.

"When did you get here?"

"Weeks ago... Almost a month."

"How come I haven't seen you before?"

"I did my shopping here last week. Your colleague helped me then."

"Is that so?" he nods and produces two bottles from under the bed.

I rush back with the beer.

"What's eating these booze peddlers? If you don't patronize them every day, they get upset?"

"Business has not been good for them. Lot of the residents are emigrating. The influx of newcomers has slowed to trickle. So demand is down."

Baldy has more news: the barber and his two young friends are scheduled to fly to the States next week. Curly is totally bent out of shape over these new developments. Just this morning he picked another fight with the youngies who threatened to break his neck the next time starts heckling them.

"Where's Mathman?"

"He took Teenie out to celebrate. He had his interview today. He's all set. He'll be flying next week if his fiancée sends the airline ticket in time."

"Looks like indeed they've unclogged the process," I go along with the flow of the conversation although my situation is stuck some place in a central medical administration, and waiting for a decree is sure to put me in a bitter mood. My voice probably betrays me when I ask: "Did you check the mail today? Anything for me by chance?"

"Nothing for you and nothing for me. I don't remember the last time I got word from home. True, I've not been very diligent writing home."

"I could ask the old fellow tomorrow if he wants to hire you too. The two of us working together could finish the job in no time at all. What do you say?" I look Baldy in the face after opening the second bottle of beer.

"Don't you dare! Once and for all, get it through your mind, I don't want any part of this racket! I have everything I need without having to kowtow to cheapskates and slave-drivers."

Walter is late by five minutes. He pulls up leisurely and carefully to the curb in front of me. He doesn't have to explain himself about being late, but it's his nature. His upbringing.

I work all morning without a break. It goes well and it makes me feel good. This time it's Helga who comes down to the cellar and invites me to the table.

"If this goes on for a week, I'll outgrow my clothes and there goes my profit, I'll have to buy pants and shirts," I add this little joke after thanking them for another magnificent lunch.

"I don't think you're in any danger. Not at pace you keep up in the cellar." Walter sips his coffee with satisfaction.

He descends the cellar steps at six on the dot. I have four tightly packed stacks of firewood to show him. The pile of untouched logs almost half of what it was. Helga sends me home with fried sausages for supper.

I thank her from the bottom of my heart.

It's six-thirty when I get to my room.

176

"You have mail!" Baldy yells at me from the usual evening hubbub.

My heart jumps a beat. It must be from home. I run to the mail office as fast as I can. There are only two people ahead of me in line. I hand over my Regal card when my turn comes. The cop comes back with a white business size envelope... My expectations dashed, I feel deflated, dejected; again it's not from my wife but probably from the Canadian embassy. Wonder what they have to say! I open it with shaking fingers and unfold the embossed stationary. I scan the text quickly. In essence it says the central medical committee suspects a case of TB. Further tests and examinations are ordered by a deadline. The name and address of a radiologist is included.

A whole slew of conflicting emotions and ideas run through my mind. Scare, despair, fear, and rage take turns torturing me. Can't imagine what's behind this new obstacle. The unknown, as usual, puts me into a panic, robs me of self-control and patience. Disturbing, how fast one can lose one's mental balance.

As usual, Baldy sees the problem in a different light.

"So what? Tomorrow morning you go to the given address, let them take another picture, and that's it. Stop worrying yourself. Believe me, if you had TB you wouldn't be here with the rest of us. Didn't you have a physical subsequent to your release from the holding tank? "

"Yes, I did. But even then I already had a stabbing pain in my chest."

"That's something else. Didn't the doctor tell you it had to do with your mind and not your lungs?"

No lights out tonight. It's another one of those nights. It keeps me not only awake but alert. I'm totally exhausted and yet can't get a wink of sleep. I keep staring at the ceiling.

Anxiety builds its towers inside me.

* * * *

Walter shrugs off my apologies in the morning and offers to give me a ride to the doctor in the city. He's simply acting on the letter from the embassy without asking for personal details.

We're already in the heart of the city when he speaks about it, but it comes out more like an expression of sympathy rather than curiosity.

"Do you think it's something serious, my boy?"

"I hope not," I'm unable to appreciate his concern, I'm depleted of words.

Among the shingles posted by the entrance I spot the one bearing the name of the assigned doctor.

I ring the bell by the doctor's door on the third floor. A woman in a white smock answers the door. Twice she goes over the letter from the embassy before asking for my patience while she talks to the doctor.

"The doctor says he can see you now if you're ready, but the fee must be paid in advance. Do you have cash on hand?" she gives me a suspicious look.

"How much are we talking about?"

"One minute, let me make sure."

While waiting I get my wallet out and count my money again even though I know exactly how much I have.

"Here we go," she hands me the bill.

Now I must really look sick, because she sounds worried: "Any problems?"

"No, no problem at all," I get hold of my wallet again, separate out two one-hundred bills and hand over the rest of the wad without counting it again.

There's a red light in the X-ray room. I'm told to strip to the waist and lie still on the white sheet of the examination bench and let the machine over me do its work, clicking, clanging, buzzing and walking to and fro.

Then I spend some time in semi-stupor in the waiting room until they call me. The doctor is ready to speak to me.

"We did a CT scan of your lungs," the doctor starts explaining while attaching three newspaper-sized film negatives to the illuminated surface on the wall. "The right lobe has two small vacuoles in a calcified state. These formed long, long time ago, fifteen or twenty years ago. Completely healed. In addition, I see a veil most likely due to a cold, but that should clear up in a few weeks."

"So I don't have TB?"

"No, not now, but you had viral pneumonia in your childhood, and what we see is the slight damage left behind."

"In other words, there's nothing to hold up my immigration to Canada?"

"Nothing at all. We'll send over the pictures to the central medical institute, and unless they have other questions you should have all your entry permit ready in days."

The meaning of his words already puts me into joyous delirium even before they all leave his lips.

Yes, yes! I've made it! I want to shout out loud, but I have to force myself to act calm and collected. I have to pretend to listen to the formalities the doctor delivers; I cannot concentrate on the formal phrases, they flow over my head, turning into ether.

"You seem to be happy with the results," Walter remarks when I finally get back to the car, obviously with a beaming face.

"Yes, thank you. sir," I sit back in the passenger seat with relief, "and please excuse the long delay."

On the way to work I relate the whole story from beginning to end. Happy end!

It's well past lunch time when we get back. Helga's waiting for us with the table set for another nice meal.

When Walter shows up in the cellar at six, I offer to keep working till eight to make up for the time lost in the city. In any case, I don't have anything better to do.

* * * *

Baldy listens to my account of the morning's adventures in silence, sunken deep in thought.

179

It doesn't take a mind reader to divine his thoughts; he's obviously upset by the prospect of being left behind, alone.

I, too, will miss him. Fate has brought us together only for a short period of time, but I've grown accustomed to his defiantly uncouth manners, his forthrightness, his obstinacy.

Mathman strides in, grinning from ear to ear.

"Feast your eyes on this, fellows. Triple X-rated, strictly for those over eighteen years of age. Are you boys sure you've passed that age?"

"Come on, let me see them," Baldy tears the photos from Mathman's hands.

He turns them over, lingering over each. Now and then he snickers like a naughty teenager.

"Where did you take these pictures?"

"Can't you tell?"

"No."

"Right here in my bunk. Don't you see the white sheets? Wait a minute, I didn't remember this one!" he laughs out loud on seeing one of the photos.

"Immediately after we came down from detention! And he managed to smuggle Teenie in here!"

"Back in mythological times," Mathman elaborates.

"This Teenie, she's quite a gal, her boobs are divine, and she shaves her cute little pussy. Quality material. I envy you!" Baldy returns the pack of photos to its owner.

"And don't I get to take look?" I act peevish.

"You're a married man, it's not right for you," Mathman sinks the photo envelop in his pocket with mock righteousness and then takes it out again for me. "Maybe you should immortalize Nina in a similar manner… You can borrow the camera," he keeps talking while watching my reaction to the pictures. He seems to enjoy his running commentary more than the looking. "And then in bed, don't let these images lead you into temptation and start playing with yourself."

"What did the sales ladies say in the photo shop where you had the film developed?" I ask him interrupting his laugh attack.

"Their eyes were aglow."

"That's all?"

"They were still in shock, mostly from seeing my cock. I'm sure they made extra copies of it."

Getting under the blanket I cannot shoo away the images from an inner screen in my mind, and indeed I suffer hunger pains for sex.

I'm making inroads into the job. Walter seems happy. Helga's cooking is fabulous. My mood though is variable.

"Walter, sir, since I left home, I have not had any communication with my family. Would it be possible to order an international call on your phone and you could deduct the cost from my pay?"

Helga gets very emotional.

"Poor boy," she says with tears in her eyes.

I go back to the cellar with a heavy heart. The lady at the telephone exchange didn't hold out much hope for me.

At six in the evening Walter takes me back to the Regal. He's almost as upset by our failure to reach my family as I am. We agree to try again Monday.

The Regal gate is fortified with three armed guards. They demand to see my card. Each of them examines it carefully.

"Where are you coming from?" one asks me harshly.

"From work."

"Where?"

"Here in the suburbs, with an elderly family. They provide the transportation."

"What time did you leave the Regal?"

"Around seven-thirty in the morning and I just got back."

"Okay," he says and enters my name in a notebook before he returns my card.

All this time a line of three forms behind me. When I move on I can hear the guards ask the same questions.

Something happened today. Something bad, obviously. I wonder what? What's the bad news tonight?

I happen to walk into Baldy on the wide outside stairs. He's smoking a cigarette.

"When did you take up the habit?" I'm surprised. I've never seen him with a cigarette in his mouth.

"Don't go up," he looks very somber. "The CSI unit is still at work. There are five of them.

"What's up?"

"They locked up Curly in one of these metal cabinets and dumped him from the third floor."

"How is he?"

"Died of shock."

"From the third floor?"

"Apparently they disabled him and dragged him up there."

"Who did?"

"They don't say yet, but suspicion points to the barber and his two pals."

"That doesn't make sense. They argued a lot, heckled each other, perhaps there was genuine hatred between them, but I don't see those young ones capable of such brutality."

"You were not there most of the time, you didn't see what was going on in the room."

"But why now? On the eve of their emigration? Are you sure you got the story right?"

"Well, all the signs add up."

"What signs?"

"The barber and his cohorts cannot prove where they were at the time of the murder."

"Where do they say they were?"

"They claim they were around, in the Regal. But I didn't see them in the room, and they all three claim they were asleep."

"Tell me what happened."

"There were only five of us earlier this afternoon. Me, Curly and the barber with his two pals. The barber threatened Curly that he'd take him out if he started heckling just once more. Curly was upset, restlessly pacing the room and then the hallway for a while before returning to the room. It kind of irritated me at the beginning, but the others lay back on their bunk. In the meantime, I too fell asleep. When I woke up they were gone."

"How do you know? Did you check their bunks?"

"No, but I was already awake when they marched into the room with great racket. "

"Did you ask them what happened?"

"They said they were out in the washroom. An hour later the cops broke into the room. They took us all to the detention center for questioning."

"And you testified against them?"

"Don't you understand I only told them what happened?" Baldy yells at me.

"Did you mention the earlier altercation, that they threatened Curly?"

"Yes, of course, I told them everything that happened."

"You shouldn't have."

"Why not?"

"Baldy, sometimes you act like a child! This was not the first altercation or heated argument among them, was it?"

"No, it wasn't."

"It wasn't the first time they warned Curly to shut up?"

"No."

"In that case why are you so sure that while you were taking a nap they managed to drag Curly out of this room and up one floor higher, stuff him in a cabinet and throw him out the window?"

"I did not state that, it only seemed reasonable."

"It's enough to sow the seed of suspicion, it'll immediately give the cops a direction in which to run off with their investigation."

"What makes you say that? Are you a police detective?"

"Come now." I try to laugh it off. "It stands to reason; if I have a group of suspects with a common thread, all I have to do is follow it to the end."

"You're right, I made a mistake. I should've kept my mouth shut. I should've spared my words when answering questions. 'I don't know. I didn't look. I was asleep. I'm not sure.

183

Could've happened like that. Possible. I didn't notice.' I should've talked like this."

"Precisely. The whole story would've sounded quite different."

"Yeah, but when the police picked us up I didn't know what'd happened. The cops didn't say anything about a murder, they just jumped all over me. The other thing was they questioned each of us separately. If I'd known about Curly's death, I would've chosen my words more carefully. Believe me, I wanted to do the right thing."

"You may have led them into a blind alley, giving the real perps a chance to get away."

"I can't deny it... That too may indeed be in the cards. There's nothing I can do about it now; I've signed my statement."

We're still standing on the wide stairs, Baldy looking down and I looking up. He's chain-smoking now, so distracted that sometimes he doesn't realize he's blowing smoke straight at me and I get a coughing fit.

Eventually, there's some movement upstairs. Four uniformed men come through the door and emerge into the light at the top of the stairs. One of then turns back to the fifth who then joins the group. We're too far to hear what they're saying; we catch only fragmentary phrases from them as they descend. Baldy, noticing the eyes fixed on something behind him, turns around. But there's no public announcement, no further news.

Slowly the policemen walk past us. One of them glances in our direction, and seems to recognize Baldy, but they keep going without a word to us.

Silence in the dorm room, unaccustomed silence. Both the tv set and radio are turned off. At the table in the middle some of the residents are eating cold cuts and bread from wrapping papers.

Mathman is lying on his back with his hands clasped behind his head, his eyes focused on something far away. Wiseman steps over to my bunk to ask if I heard about today's events. Whiskers joins us too.

Only Baldy stays away.

For a while the desultory conversation continues without any new information being added. No one knows where the barber and his pals are.

Tonight again Helga packed a supper for me, but I don't feel like opening it, I stow the plastic shopping bag in the refrigerator.

There's no way of getting away from the lights suspended from the ceiling. They burn through my eyelids, deep into my brain. They keep doing that long after to world around me ceases to exist.

Whiskers shakes my shoulder to wake me up with a message from Blondie: I promised Father Petri to accompany him to a mass in a nearby village. At first I cannot make any sense of the message, so groggy I am with sleep.

"You promised Father Petri…"

"Okay, okay," I seem to recall something we said on parting last Sunday. My God, another week's passed? The thought brings me back to full consciousness. "What time is it?"

"Eight-thirty."

I crawl out of bed but have no desire to go anywhere. Can't make up my mind one way or the other and stay standing by the bunk, paralyzed. Mathman is snoring softly. Returning from the washroom I work up enough energy to visit the chapel. Father Petri is out in the corridor talking to an elderly lady. He catches sight of me and signals for me to wait.

"Praise the Lord!" he turns to me when the lady leaves.

"Forever and ever, amen."

"How're you faring, my son?" he looks at me with sadness.

"Not too well after yesterday's events."

"Yes, I know what you mean," he nods. "I got the news this morning, as soon as I got here. We live in a violent world, my son."

"Yes, Father."

"Are you ready to go?"

"I'd like to postpone this trip till next Sunday. I don't really feel up to it now, Father."

"I understand. However, next week my duty will take me some other place. I'll send a word."

Relieved, I set out in the direction of the female barracks. Cold weather is back again. The advance winds of winter are exploring the anemic sunlight.

The latest mortality seems to dampen my spirit. Last night Baldy informed me that the broken pieces of the cabinet were still lying on the ground near the building, but this morning I didn't think of leaning out the window to look for them.

I wonder why?

Blondie glares at me with a questioning look when I enter their room.

"Didn't you go with Father Petri?"

"A change of plans."

"But you promised."

"We met, talked it over, and parted amicably just minutes ago."

"Oh, well, then it's all right. I was worried that you had forgotten or Whiskers neglected to give you the message."

"No, he didn't. He woke me this morning with it."

"I hear they killed someone again."

"Someone from our dorm room."

"Whiskers forgot to mention that detail."

"He didn't know at the time," Teenie joins us at the table. "Hello everyone! I got away a little earlier last night from that god-damned joint. I told the boss I'd go in at noon today to clean up the mess, but I just couldn't stay a moment longer, and he had to let me get off ahead closing time. Lo and behold, wonders will never cease! He let me go! But I didn't get much sleep. I kept having these nightmares about monsters. I woke up completely wrung out, without a drop of energy."

"You dream about monsters?"

"Yes, I dream of monsters. What kind of characters you think surround me all night? Angels? Some of them could give you a heart attack just by looking at you. Just imagine running into someone like that in a dark street late at night! I'd be frightened to death on the spot."

"Come now, you can make up the most fantastic stories!" Blondie snaps back.

"Who? Me?" Teenie turns on her.

"Okay, girls, break it up! Stop this catfight. Why don't you brew coffee instead?" I put in my two pennies.

"It's your turn," Teenie points to Blondie.

Blondie gets up with a frown, gathers the coffee mugs, the spoons and the water pot and ambles out to the washroom.

"Do you know where your holier-than-thou girl is?" Teenie asks when the two of us are alone.

"Who're you talking about?"

"You know who! Nina."

"Isn't she here?"

"This evening her prince came on a white horse and took her away to his pleasure palace. What do you say to that?"

I can feel my face turn hot from the blood flooding it.

"You're a real asshole. You should've had her. You should've swept her off her feet and stuck it to her. But you want to act like a gentleman. You value gestures, sweet nothings, sentiment. Fifty times you were getting a nervous breakdown about her, wooing her, begging her, while someone else came, scooped her up from her bed where the princess was resting her ass all day because working was beneath her dignity, and in spite of her protestations he abducted her from this hellhole and they rode off into the blue yonder."

"Who rode off?" Blondie just stepped in on the last words.

"Ninotchka."

"You telling the story of last night's party? Don't make such big eyes about it!" Blondie has trouble talking over a laughing fit. "It's not worth a shrug. They're all like that. They come here wiggling their fannies and then move on. There's no soul in them. They play the innocent virgin, collect sympathy and

187

then they sneak off with the first nobody who happens to come along with a hard on. Don't you fret about her, you're better off whacking off in the washroom. For that you need no heart, no heartache, no conscience, only fantasy. We have a little strong stuff to go with the coffee, Teenie's present."

She pours out the stuff into shot glasses. The aroma of brandy roams around my head.

After the first reaction settles I don't remain stirred up by the news about Nina. What I feel is quiet resignation, bitterness mixed with pain, the almond taste of failure.

By the time coffee is served Mathman enters with Whiskers in tow.

"I swear I've had it up to here with the Regal, screw it. Did you know the cops picked up Baldy again, screw it?" he sits down next to me.

"Not arrested?"

"Good question, screw it. Because he was wagging his tongue too much, screw it."

"Yes, yes, but how was he to know what to say? At the time they questioned him he had no idea what had happened to Curly," I feel obligated to come to Baldy's defense and do so in no uncertain terms.

"You're right, screw it, let's forget the whole thing."

"On the other hand, the barber and his confederates are still in custody," adds Mathman, but then he leans toward his girl. "It's six or half a dozen to me. Next week I'll be flying. How about it, Teenie? Will you see me off to the bus? Will you say goodbye to your old friend?"

Sudden silence descends over the table. Everyone turns inward, calculating his or her own chances.

The door opens. Nina walks in. She seems stunned by the silence of the crowded table. She bends her head. Trying to hide a blush. She heads for her bunk.

"Did you have a walloping big skin session, screw it?" Whiskers yells after her.

"My friends, I've got to run, see you around," I rise quickly. I don't want to witness another provocation.

As soon as I close the door behind me, I hear Mathman's horselaugh.

He couldn't care less, he only has a few more days to endure here.

Just as I step out of the building, I hear running footsteps behind me. Teenie's, as it turns out

"I'd like to talk to you," she's breathless, "but not here, let's go for a walk."

"I left because…"

"I know, I know. I don't like the blunt language Whiskers uses. But it's something else I have on my mind."

The streetlamp by the walkway lights up Teenie's face, bringing out an expression of anxiety in high relief.

"I can see you, too, have your problems," I choose to speak bluntly, just to make easier for her to get started.

"Yes, I've gotten myself into trouble. At the beginning I thought it was to be nothing but a passing adventure, but as time went on I found myself falling for Mathman more and more. In my case, like in yours, sex is not just another thing to do like brushing teeth. I enjoyed having a steady partner; it was convenient but not enough. Blondie mentioned to you that we both came from an orphanage. I never knew my parents; I grew up like a wildflower. That's why I fled communism; if it's a goose, let it be fat. I had no family, no one back home, nothing to keep me from trying my luck abroad."

"So you fell in love With Mathman."

"Yes, deeper and deeper."

"He's not a committed partner. I suspect you've aware of some of his heroic exploits."

"I don't care about his sex affaires, I'm not the jealous type."

"He's engaged."

"Others have been, too."

"He's on his way to her, she's paying his fare, she's counting on him marrying her."

"Yes, that's all true, I know the situation. But I'm pregnant, and Mathman is my baby's father."

"Does he know?"

"No, not yet. I have not made up my mind yet."

"Teenie, there's nothing to think over. You can bear a hundred babies for him; he'll never stay with you."

"Am I not worthy of him?"

"No, that's not the point. He's an impulsive, adventurous, bohemian spirit, has no mind for commitment. Be realistic! You're looking to start a family, you want love, security, a well-balanced life, everything you missed in your childhood. You'll never get any of these from him."

"What do you suggest?"

"Wouldn't hurt to sit down with him and talk it over."

"That's exactly what I want to avoid."

"Good Heavens, then what?"

"I'll keep the child, and I'll raise it alone."

"Alone? Where? On what?"

"I have a job now, I can earn a living, I'll find a way."

"Yes, but how will that work when there are two of you? Who's going to be with the kid while you're at work? Teenie, come to your senses. You haven't got a chance, no matter how mulish you're going to be about it."

"I haven't got a chance to have what? Struggle, hardship? So what? That's been my life all along. It's not going to get any worse."

"Your sacrifice doesn't make any sense. Do you want the same kind of life for your child that you've had? How could you wish that on anyone?"

"You're evil, cruel!" she starts bawling convulsively. "I trusted you, I thought you were different from the others. But now I see you think the same way as Mathman!"

"Because I refuse to say the things you expect from me?"

"Forget the whole thing, forget I ever talked to you. I'll find a way somehow."

"I suggest you go to our medical officer and ask him for advice. And listen to what he has to say." I try consoling her with my arms around her, but she pushes me away and runs off.

I resume my walk with a heavy heart.

The trees of the park beyond the walkway nod toward me in a solemn pose as if expressing their agreement with me. The irrepressible question arises in my mind: What kind of passion drives us always into the middle of a roiling ocean?

I find Baldy standing in the corridor with eyes scanning the passersby.

"I've been waiting for you," he says with palpable relief. "Let's go out and get some fresh air."

"Tell me what's going on. Why did they pull you in again?" I wait asking him until we're out in the courtyard.

"Would you believe it? The barber and his two associates claimed in their confession that I was in on the caper and I only backed out in the last minute. I walked away from them."

"From where?"

"According to their story there were four of us when we grabbed Curly, but after we dragged him out to the corridor, I got cold feet and snuck off."

"Devils," I whisper to myself.

"What's that?"

"It's a devilish plot. They try to spread the blame. Make it look like mob action. If they're in a pickle they want others to share it with. Next thing they'll make you the ringleader."

"That's why they questioned me again," Baldy's face is turned to the ground.

"Did the three suspects confess to the crime?"

"Looks like to me they did, because they were in pretty bad shape the last time I saw them, which was about half an hour ago. I think all three of them had been subjected to very vigorous interrogation."

"And how about you?"

"Just take a look at me!"

We continue walking side by side without another word being exchanged for another half an hour.

When we open the door to the dorm room we find the usual Babel, the usual commotion, the usual ear-piercing noise.

191

Life reasserts itself, returns to its natural course. Nature heals itself fast. For the first time since yesterday I feel hungry again.

I wake up well-rested in the following morning. I rush out but end up having to wait for Walter, I'm too early at the Work Plaza. Standing there, I try to assess the situation, the labor market.

There are nine of us on display, for hire.

So far no customers.

Only a thin sigh roams among us.

* * * *

I can't seem to perk up and wield the axe with the same enthusiasm I had last week. Walter comes down twice this morning to check on me, but makes no comment on my progress or the lack thereof. It's only at the lunch table he gets down to business: at this rate I'm not going to finish the job by tomorrow, I'll need another day. I assure him I'll gather more strength and shift into higher gear.

"Don't rush it, boy, we have time. And we can squeeze it out of our pension income."

I can't thank him for his kindness; my mind is on the telephone, I focus all my attention and energy on trying to activate the inert object with sheer willpower. First thing this morning we placed a call to my family. But no response so far.

After a strong coffee I feel strength seep back into my limbs. I stop moping and futzing; instead, I watch the direction and the effect of the whacks. My productivity is a good measure of my spirit; the split logs quickly build up into a wall.

At six in the evening Walter drops me off in front of the Regal.

"Get some rest, boy," he pats my shoulder.

When I turn back to say goodnight, I find him still staring at the bleak building, lost in thought behind the steering wheel.

I'm in no mood to go up to the dorm room. I stall in the courtyard. It's a few degrees warmer than yesterday and less windy. Then suddenly I realize I have a good reason to linger here: the bulletin board. It's only a short walk to it. There are only two people perusing it. I can hardly believe my eyes; there are eight long emigrations lists posted. Groups are scheduled for Wednesday, Thursday, and Friday. I scan the lists of the lucky ones without emotion, objectively like a historical document. Next I take a look at the list of mail recipients. My name is among them.

I will not make a spectacle of myself, nor will I wreck my nerves by arriving at the post cubicle out of breath; I'll make my way there without undue haste; cautious optimism swirls in my mind.

At first a flash of white in the clerk's hand almost shoves me back into the abyss of despair, but then I recognize my wife's handwriting on it.

It's only a two-page letter.

I hardly finish reading it when I start reading it again. They got the greeting card, but the package has not reached them yet. The boys are well, but they miss me a lot. She, too, is fine, her spirit is up; however, she's not been working for the past week. Of course, she gives no reason. My parents are all right. My father had bad cold, more severe than usual, but he's over the worst of it. The neighbors, too, send their regards. Everyone is prepared to get good news from me. She knows I tried calling her, but every time she answered the line went dead. And she misses me beyond belief.

On the way up I run into Wiseman. He looks at me with undisguised contempt.

"I remember the resolution I made. But then this trouble intervened, I got a job again this week to make up for the loss of last week, but when I'm done, I'll hit the books," I make a full confession before he can dump on me again.

"Do you really believe what you're saying? I don't any more. Your word is worthless to me," he renders the final verdict with lukewarm disgust.

"You know what? I don't give a crap what you think. I've had enough of you and your sanctimonious attitude," I can hold my peace no longer. "You talk as if I spent all day chasing clouds and not money!"

"That's the problem!"

"My first a foremost problem is to provide for the family I left behind. Have you seen Baldy?"

"He was here this afternoon. He could've run out for something."

"Any news of the barber and his pals?"

"Nothing. They're under arrest."

I treat myself to a supper from Helga's bag. It's beef goulash leftover from lunch. Beer would go well with it, but I don't trust that bootlegger on the third floor. I can do without him. I wash the meal down with water from the faucet in the washroom.

I pass the time just sitting around till nine, waiting for Baldy. But he doesn't show up.

Before I finally fall asleep, I come awake several times and look over to his bunk to see if he's back yet.

* * * *

Before going to work I stop by Baldy's bunk to see if he's awake. He's quietly lying there turned to the wall; impossible to tell if his eyes are open. I put a hand on his shoulder, but there's no reaction.

Walter greets me in high spirits. Today is his birthday. There's going to be a party at noon, a neighbor is going to be there. His voice is louder, talks more. The usual pensive expression on his face has been replaced by a beaming smile. His good mood is infectious; even I begin to feel better. I give him the good news, a letter from home.

"Do you have a photo of your family?" he asks with sparkles in his eyes.

194

"Unfortunately, no. But I'll write to my wife, ask her for a family photo, and if I'm still here I'll show it to you."

At noon I estimate I could finish the job by eight or nine if I skip Walter's party and put my back into the job. And I remember that in the celebratory mood in the morning we forgot to put in an order for the phone call. Walter makes a devil-may-care gesture saying we put off everything till tomorrow.

The guests regard me as if I had come from Mars. I accidentally overhear a brief exchange between one of them and Helga.

"My dear, do you trust this footloose foreigner from the Regal? Doesn't he steal?"

"Oh, come now!" Helga pipes up. "He's not only honest but a hard worker. A little later I'll take you down to the cellar and show you what good work he's done. We bring home a woodcutter from the Regal every year, but we never had anyone as devoted and careful as he is."

The party goes on until three-thirty. It's only then that I start my afternoon shift. But I feel too mellow from too much eating and drinking. Mostly the latter.

In spite of my protestation Walter calls a taxi after six and sends me home.

I spy Baldy's figure on the walkway that circles the courtyard. I yell out to him, but he doesn't even turn around. I have to run to catch up with him.

"What's happened to you, didn't you hear me calling to you?" I grab him by the arm.

"Yeah, is that you?" he hesitates before turning to me.

I can't see his eyes but I smell alcohol on his breath.

"You been drinking?"

"So what?"

"I had supper waiting for you last night, where did you disappear to?"

"I had something to take care of."

"What kind of an answer is that, Baldy?"

195

"What kind, what kind indeed… Why don't you leave me alone? Why bother?"

I put an arm around his back and drag him toward the entrance. At first he resists, tries to shake my arm loose, but then he settles down and quietly walks with me, albeit with uncertain steps.

By the time we make it up to the room he becomes very heavy. He's really plastered. It's best to help him to his bunk. Wiseman is there as usual, buried in his books. I ask him to help.

We take Baldy's shoes and coat off. He doesn't let us pull his sweater off. Eventually, we just lay him down fully dressed.

He doesn't open his mouth for the rest of the day.

I place my supper in the refrigerator. I ask about Mathman and Whiskers, but no one has seen them.

I head for the female dormitory. Three cops coming from the opposite direction on the walkway. They stop me. Want to see my ID card. They beam a flashlight in my eyes and then let me go. This the first time I've been asked to ID myself within the Regal.

I find all four of them at the table caught up in a fierce card game.

"Hi there," Mathman catches me from the corner of his eye, "Watch the way I deal with this band of amateurs!" he speaks with his usual high energy as he slams an ace on top of the card pile in the middle of the table. "Well, what did I say?" he bellows triumphantly.

"Wait a minute! Where did you get that ace from? The ace of clubs went out a minute ago!" Teenie screeches.

"That's right, screw it," Whiskers rummages through the pile of cards, and in seconds he comes up with another ace of clubs, "here it is, screw it, look at it, the real ace of clubs."

"You're a disgusting cheat! You've been cheating all along, haven't you? We should cut his balls off," Blondie screams at him.

"Wait a minute! Quiet please!" I step into the fracas. "If you knew he was a cardsharp why did you sit down to play with him?"

"What makes you think you're so smart?" Teenie jumps all over me.

"Have I ever sat down with you people for a game of cards? No! Never! So why pick on me?"

"Let's drop it!" Whiskers throws the cards on the table. "Teenie, see if you can dig up some booze!"

I report the good news: letter from home. Blondie wants to see it. When she's finished reading it she hands it to Whiskers. The letter goes around the table.

"The only thing that's missing is that XOXOXOXOXO," I mention in jest.

"An Australian custom," Mathman grins. "My pussycat ends all her letters with such sweet nothings."

"When did you get this one?" Whiskers points to the letter.

"I picked it up last night."

"In that case you have another letter today. I saw it this afternoon on the board."

"You must be thinking of yesterday's mail."

"Run over there and check it out."

"So what are you waiting for?" Blondie pokes me with a finger.

What indeed! Next thing I know I'm galloping to the bulletin board.

I quickly scan the list. My name! It's there!

The embossed envelope yields its secret: a twice-folded sheet of paper to fit the business-sized envelope.

"We are glad to inform you that you have met our conditions for immigration.

"Please accept our congratulations! We wish you success in your new homeland. Your travel will be arranged. We have ordered an airline ticket in your name for a flight of Canadian Airlines. You will receive it at the airport..."

I read it and reread it two more times in quick succession.

As far as I know joy does not scratch one's throat; therefore, I must have something else happening to me.

I hurry back to the girls.

"Look, Mathman, you'll be flying Friday, and Wednesday next week it'll be my turn!" I wave the letter in his face like a flag.

Teenie grabs the sheet of paper from my hand and reads it.

"It's true," she says sadly as tears run down her cheeks.

I make an attempt at waking Baldy, so that we could celebrate the great news together, but he's dead to this world again tonight.

Sleep evades me all night long. Closing my eyes doesn't help. I keep tossing and turning in my bed, just as thoughts keep tossing and turning inside my head.

Some moments I fall into such despair, I feel totally empty inside, as if someone had wiped me clean of all my memories. And now, deprived of my past, I'm lying here with nothing but small clumps of hope in my soul.

An eraser wielded by happiness, that's the image I invent to elucidate this emptiness inside me. Rhapsodic tatters of thoughts project themselves, hopping back and forth, but I have no control over them, I can't put them in order and make sense out of them. In the final analysis I have no idea what's wrong with me or my present situation. The time served here in limbo has completely entangled inside me everything I thought was me, because at the Regal I never had a quiet moment to work through the events happening to me or around me. Such an orderly process of filtering, purifying, crystallizing my experiences was impossible, because they followed one another in such quick succession and under such hellish circumstances that none of them left a clear thought behind; not one idea seared itself into the skin of my memory just so that I could feel the pain caused by its red-hot brand and sense the smell of sizzling time in my roasting flesh. One thing is clear: from now on I belong to the camp of those who are fleeing from here. That's what I should be celebrating, but the spring of my sentiments has run dry, from its depths not one little drop can form.

I keep tossing and turning all night without finding my place.

Inevitably, dawn-time arousal finds its way, it attacks me in wave after wave, wrecking my already weakened nerves.

A fairytale vision of Nina's body drizzles colors on my mood and liberates the passion so long kept under control by my consciousness. The memory of old love affairs hurry to my help.

* * * *

Still the morning of my escape from the Regal is beset with birthing pains. I feel like reaching out and pulling it into light, but my efforts are defeated by a sudden and deep sleep that overcomes me.

Colorful visions crowd my view. It feels good to be surrounded by them.

Eventually the visions coalesce into a dream that foretells my long-awaited departure in vivid details, most of them obviously expectable, except for one, just a flash that stands out among them as truly dreamlike.

Baldy sees me off to the bus. He carries my small brown bag that had crossed the border with me.

The huge white transport vehicle rests majestically in one corner of the Regal courtyard. When we walk up to it Baldy hands me my meager luggage.

"Take care of yourself!"

Others are gathering on the walkway. All waiting for some kinds of a signal to crowd into the bus.

From the morning glow a hand reaches out.

It points out the direction.

"Let us know when you get to Canada," Baldy pulls his mouth into the shape of a smile.

"You too keep in touch!" I give him a hug.

"This is our farewell?" he stands at the edge of the tumult, looking after me as I blend into the crowd.

I have one foot on the step leading into the bus when someone thrashes her way through the travelers, throws her arms around my neck and presses her hot lips against mine. I can taste her tongue, I can revel in the confluence of our saliva, I can feel her heart throb and her pointed nipples poke through my shirt to tease my skin.

"From the first moment it was you I wanted. Forgive me for not becoming yours!"

The silk of her whisperings caresses my ears.

In the same flashing way she appeared, in the next moment she suddenly detaches herself and runs off into vaporous nothingness where there's no flesh, no morning, no courtyard, no sky above us and no ground under our feet; from there she yells after me: "Tamas, I love you!"

Footnotes:
The unidentified quotes in the second encounter with Father Petri are from Aeneas by Virgil, Book VI, pp 7-8 and Letter XXVIII by Seneca

Comments by German Critics:

Zoltán Böszörményi's story of escape largely takes place in a Western European detention camp and speaks not only about the feeling of confinement, violent deaths, desperation and the hope of getting accepted in a peaceful country but also of tenderly sprouting love affairs and friendship.
Hans-Henning Paetzke
Literatursalon von Unger, Berlin

True-to life psychodrama of refugee life in detention camps.

This thematically timely, tightly written and fluently translated book rises above the time and place of its story, overarching a situation of existential threat that leaves escape as the only alternative.
Elke Mehnert
(Stacheldraht)

A society broken into isolated individuals can justly claim the attention of the potential reader.
Gabriella Kinda
(Ostragehege)

This book often reminds us of today's refugee stories: the impossibility of staying at home, the fear and the dangers involved in the escape and then the unfriendly or indifferent reception followed by scrapes, frayed nerves, even violence in the camp. Add to that unceasingly germinating hope, the overwhelming joy over finding a new home—only to be overshadowed by doubts about the future and soul-torturing thoughts about family left behind.
Gudrun Brzoska
(Deutsch-Ungarische Zeitschrift Unsere Post and Stacheldraht)

ABOUT THE AUTHOR

Zoltán Böszörményi, a Hungarian poet and writer, crossed the Iron Curtain in the 80's in frenetic escape as a budding poet, but since the regime change, he has often returned, resumed his writing carrier and published extensively, not only in Hungarian but also in translation. Two of his novels are available in English: "Far from Nothing" (Exile Editions, Canada, 2006) and "The Club at Eddie's Bar" (Phaeton Press, Ireland, 2013).

Made in the USA
Middletown, DE
25 May 2019